· Pueblo Architecture and Modern Adobes ·

Pueblo Architecture and Modern

The Residential Designs of William Lumpkins

Adobes

By Joseph Traugott

Museum of New Mexico Press
Santa Fe

Project editor: Mary Wachs
Design and production: Susan Surprise
Set in Adobe Bembo and Caslon Open Face.

Manufactured in Hong Kong.

10 9 8 7 6 5 4 3 2 1

Library of Congress Cataloging-in-Publication Data

Traugott, Joseph.
    Pueblo Architecture and Modern Adobes : the residential designs of William Lumpkins / by Joseph Traugott ; with a foreword by William Lumpkins.
        p.   cm.
    Includes bibliographical references.
    ISBN 0-89013-368-9 (c).—ISBN 0-89013-367-0 (p).
    1. Lumpkins, William T.—Themes, motives.   2. Adobe houses—Southwest, New.   3. Pueblo architecture—Influence.   4. Architecture and solar radiation—Southwest, New.   I. Lumpkins, William T.   II. Title.
    NA737.L85A4   1998
    728'.092—dc21   98-4201
                                                                        CIP

MUSEUM OF NEW MEXICO PRESS
Post Office Box 2087
Santa Fe, New Mexico 87504

· CONTENTS ·

MY PUEBLO-BASED DRAWINGS investigate the visual forms and organizational principles developed by Pueblo builders over many centuries. The amazing utility
and strength of their buildings constitute a strong part of America's architectural
heritage. Now, after more than thirty years, the publication of these drawings will
enable a new generation to reinterpret the contributions of Pueblo architecture
and adapt their lessons to modern southwestern design. Could these designs be
built today? Yes! Any good builder could produce them; it just takes a team of
skilled craftsmen.

—BILL LUMPKINS,
SANTA FE, APRIL 1998

FOR MORE THAN six decades New Mexicans have known Bill Lumpkins (b. 1909) as both an artist and an architect. Ironically, many who think of Lumpkins as an important southwestern architect are unaware of his work as a contemporary artist, and the reverse also is true. Yet both kinds of visual thinking have informed his creative activities in mutually supportive ways.

Early in the 1930s, Lumpkins grounded his architecture in "honesty, simplicity, and usefulness,"[1] the fundamental principles of the Craftsman aesthetic promoted by Gustav Stickley in his magazine *The Craftsman*. Stickley pitched his rejection of industrial life and industrially made products to a "better class" of farmers who "own their farms, skilled workers in cities, and artisans who rejected factory work."[2] The appeal encouraged a nostalgic glorification of preindustrial, handmade objects over machinemade goods. Stickley strove for self-sufficiency in an era of increasing social complexity and interaction.

The images of craftsman homes and furnishings that Stickley published in *The Craftsman* underscored the importance of courtyards, fireplaces, benches, pergolas, gardens, partition walls, and multilevel designs. Stickley promoted handwrought details as the core of his attitudes toward architecture and interior design. He lauded the use of simple materials and encouraged the inclusion of wooden beams, wainscoting, bookcases, cabinets, and built-in benches in craftsman-built homes.

FIGURE 1.
The mission at Acoma served as
an important architectural icon
in the development of the
revival of Spanish Colonial
architectural forms. The shadows
cast by the building reinforce
the concepts of religious and
architectural wholeness. Lumpkins uses shadows in a different
manner, to fracture his designs
and create the illusion
of multistory Pueblo buildings
developed by accretion.

Lumpkins found that these details could serve as important symbols of the ideas embedded in his architecture and incorporated them into the Pueblo-based conceptual projects that constitute this book.

Craftsman attitudes played an important role in the development of an architectural revival in New Mexico early in the twentieth century. The traditional use of earth, stone, and timber found in New Mexico Pueblo and Hispanic homes exemplified many of the attitudes that Stickley sought to re-create through the Arts and Crafts movement. Ironically, the movement vanished on the East and West coasts just as it blossomed in the Southwest.

Promoters in New Mexico sought to capitalize on the architecture of the region beginning at the end of the nineteenth century. The development of tourist-oriented buildings along the Santa Fe Railway route encouraged preservationists' attitudes in Santa Fe. These efforts led to the "restoration" of the colonial Palace of the Governors in 1909–11 and to the development of the "Cathedral in the Desert," the New Mexico pavilion at the 1915 Panama-California Exposition in San Diego. The building combined the Spanish Colonial design of the mission church at Acoma with details borrowed from other New Mexico missions. A second, enlarged version of the pavilion became the Museum of Fine Arts of the Museum of New Mexico. This building codified what became known as the Pueblo Revival style, or the Spanish Colonial Revival style.[3]

Lumpkins had been designing what he called Spanish-Pueblo homes for three decades when he set out to experiment with this series of Pueblo-based residences. Normally he organized his Spanish-Pueblo homes around an open, central courtyard with individual rooms and activity wings radiating from the four sides of the courtyard.[4] When these designs did not include a courtyard, the layout looked as if the living room, kitchen, and dining room contracted inwardly until the central open space disappeared. In this set of Pueblo-based designs, Lumpkins broke with the basic organizational principles found in his Spanish-Pueblo designs by combining prehistoric Pueblo elements with mainstream twentieth-century attitudes.

Lumpkins investigates Pueblo architecture with a formalist methodology that is paradoxically anti-anthropological. He begins with elevations, details, and floor plans taken from the nineteenth-century archaeological studies of Victor and

Cosmos Mindeleff, wrests these ideas out of their Pueblo cultural matrix, transforms them from one material to another, and then reinserts these decontextualized ideas into the architecture of twentieth-century mainstream lifeways.

These reinterpretations are not derived from either historic or archaeological determinations of function. Instead, Lumpkins's modern designs ascribe new functions to these fixed spatial arrangements and ignore Pueblo distinctions between habitation rooms, storage rooms, and religious structures. The Craftsman aesthetic is always present as an underlying organizational principle affecting the design and choice of elements within these modern residences.

Lumpkins spends much effort defining and refining the details of his Pueblo-based conceptual drawings. At first his emphasis on small details seems to contradict the broad concepts of massing multilevel adobe forms and asymmetrical layouts. However, carefully drawn ceilings, fireplaces, doors, windows, frescos, and solar heating details affirm their conceptual importance to this project. These essential details serve as architectural signs that point toward the roots of Lumpkins's architecture in the Arts and Crafts movement, the spiritual attitudes ascribed to Pueblo culture, as well as to his own emotional responses to nature and the landscape.

A PAINTERLY AESTHETIC

LUMPKINS'S PAINTINGS OFFER important visual clues into his use of mass and form within this series of architectural designs. During the 1920s and well before beginning formal architectural training, Lumpkins began painting landscapes in southeastern New Mexico.[5] In 1931 he saw an exhibition of John Marin's modernist watercolors and was heavily influenced by their expressionist style and Cubist analysis of space. Soon the young painter began to work with elements of Marin's style, as did many other New Mexico artists during the 1930s—including Gina Knee, Charles Mattox, and Cady Wells. Lumpkins's interest in abstracted form, which he developed through his painting, provides a solid foundation for his architectural aesthetic.

In 1935 he painted his first successful nonobjective watercolors, including *This Was a Breakthru* (figure 3). This work symbolizes Lumpkins's realization that his

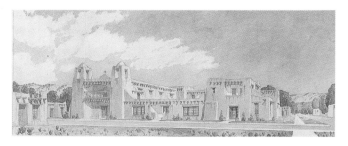

FIGURE 2.
Kenneth Chapman (1875–1968), *New Art Museum, Santa Fe—South Front*, 1916, watercolor, 11 1/2 × 28 3/8 inches, Museum of Fine Arts. Chapman's watercolor rendering of the proposed museum building captures the spirit of the early revival architecture in New Mexico. While based largely on the mission at Acoma, the design is a pastiche of facades from other churches. Note how the shadows in this revival design accentuate minor details such as balconies, vigas, and bell towers rather than the mass of the main structure.

FIGURE 3.
William Lumpkins, *This Was a Breakthru*, 1935, watercolor, 7 1/2 × 10 1/2 inches, Museum of Fine Arts.

FIGURE 4.
William Lumpkins, *Desert Arroyo*,
1938, watercolor, 14 3/4 × 21
inches, collection of Robert
Blommer and Lowell Sousie.

own expression was not limited to recognizable images. This small work layers brushstrokes as the artist layers adobe forms and builds with translucent veils of light and shadow in later architectural projects. The connections between this early abstraction and Lumpkins's experimental architectural projects demonstrate a provocative creative unity.

As Lumpkins developed his private architect practice in Santa Fe during the 1930s, he continued to work on his watercolors in his spare time. In 1935 he met Santa Fe artist Raymond Jonson, the nonobjective painter, and soon thereafter brought four of his watercolors for Jonson to see. A friendship blossomed that lasted until Jonson's death in 1982.

In 1938 Jonson and Taos painter Emil Bisttram founded the Transcendental Painting Group and included Lumpkins in this association of New Mexico modernists. During this period the members of the group discussed nonreferential art, organized exhibitions, and propagandized in favor of abstract works that engendered spiritualist responses by viewers. The group disbanded in 1942 after several members left New Mexico and others, including Lumpkins, joined the military.

Lumpkins's lifelong dedication to abstract forms and nonreferential painting strongly influences the dominance of flowing room blocks and asymmetric interior organization in his architecture. Abstraction also underscores the abandonment of formal dining and living rooms in favor of spaces with loosely structured functions. The presentation of these details helps Lumpkins's designs acquire an architectural spirituality that transcends contemporary society by referring back to preindustrial relationships between culture and the environment. From this perspective only slim distinctions separate Lumpkins's abstract art from his conceptual architecture.

Watercolors such as *Desert Arroyo* (figure 4) from 1938 reveal the abstract, asymmetric attitudes that provide the underlying aesthetic foundations for this series of Pueblo-based architectural drawings. Lumpkins presents the landscape as if it were a living form in which land and sky meld into a single force that lyrically flows through the picture plane. The organic nature of his depictions reaffirms a vision of the earth as provider and sustainer that can, in turn, be sculpted into adobe homes. Lumpkins's aesthetic outlook imbues these Pueblo-based designs with his sense of spirituality and reverence.

WILLIAM LUMPKINS'S PUEBLO-BASED RESIDENTIAL DESIGNS

IN 1965 ARCHITECT William Lumpkins left the high-pressure world of California's commercial building boom and returned to his native New Mexico for a well-needed vacation. Part of his holiday was spent at Gordon Pettit's ranch in Togeye Canyon on the southern slopes of the Zuni Mountains near Ramah, in west-central New Mexico.[6] Lumpkins had worked on commercial projects with Pettit, a real estate developer who earlier had studied anthropology and archaeology.

Lumpkins hiked through Togeye Canyon to some of the notable ruins of the area, including what was probably the Pettit site perched on the edge of a hundred-foot butte and the Kluckhohn site on the canyon floor below. Pettit himself had excavated thirty-four rooms at the site named for him and knew the archaeology of the region. The Kluckhohn site, one of the largest ruins in the vicinity, features four blocks of rooms enclosing a rectangular courtyard.[7]

Back at the ranch Lumpkins retreated to Pettit's library, where he discovered Victor Mindeleff's 1889 publication "A Study of Pueblo Architecture: Tusayan and Cibola," and his brother Cosmos Mindeleff's 1897 "Cliff Ruins of Canyon de Chelly, Arizona." The maps, floor plans, elevations, and interior illustrations fascinated Lumpkins, who asked to borrow these early studies of historic Pueblo and prehistoric Anasazi architecture. He had assumed that open rectangular courtyards were brought to New Mexico by the Spanish, yet his visit to the pre-Spanish

SOUTH PASSAGEWAY OF WALPI.

FIGURE 5.
H. Hobart Nichols, *South Passageway of Walpi*, line engraving of a pen-and-ink drawing made from a photograph (plate XXII) in Victor Mendeleff's "A Study of Pueblo Architecture."

Pueblo ruins in the Zuni Mountains revealed another time line. The formal similarities between the courtyard at Kluckhohn ruin and Spanish courtyards caused Lumpkins to rethink New Mexico architecture.

After returning to California, Lumpkins sought to distill the native architectural tradition that had been largely lost in the Spanish Colonial Revival movement. He began designing a series of modern residences based on the Pueblo design principles found in the Mindeleff publications studied at the Pettit ranch. At night, after a full day designing, engineering, and managing commercial construction projects, Lumpkins sketched ideas for his residential housing projects. In all, he designed forty-eight residential projects, each containing two sheets.[8] The first sheet presented source materials, floor plans, and elevations; the second sheet presented details and cross-section views. Each synthesized Lumpkins's dynamic interaction between anthropology, history, memory, nostalgia, and modern architectural design.

Lumpkins finished the project before he returned to New Mexico in 1967 to open an architectural practice. By the 1970s he was pioneering passive-solar adobe designs and was known as the dean of the region's solar architects.[9] In 1981 he published *Casa del Sol: Your Guide to Passive Solar House Design.* Sadly, Lumpkins's Santa Fe clients opted for conventional revival architecture based on modifications of Spanish architectural forms, and none of the Pueblo-based projects presented here advanced beyond conceptualization.

Lumpkins began designing southwestern residences in the 1930s, relying heavily on traditional Hispanic house forms and furniture to create what he termed Spanish-Pueblo designs. He borrowed heavily on experiences from the period 1932–3 when he had operated a furniture-making workshop in Peñasco, New Mexico, as part of the State of New Mexico's Department of Vocational Education programs.[10] His architectural projects of the period emphasized the use of adobe, *vigas, latillas, portals,* built-up doors, and temperature control through well-placed windows and roof overhangs.

In 1946 Lumpkins published *Modern Spanish Pueblo Homes,* a collection of his residential building plans that captured the essence of revival architecture from the prewar period but included passive heating and cooling features that distinguish

Lumpkins's early projects from those of his peers. The designs began with his first passive solar home, built near Capitan, New Mexico, in 1935.[11]

Lumpkins expanded his ideas on Spanish-Pueblo homes in *La Casa Adobe*, a 1961 publication that also offered a brief history of Hispanic house types in New Mexico. The text notes that the first Hispanic homes were based on a "Mediterranean" style, with rooms surrounding an open central courtyard with *portals*. These homes could be linked together, creating double-thick walls between units. This Mediterranean style, changed after 1840 when the internal *portals* disappeared and were replaced with a wide center hallway with rooms placed on either side. The later style included a public *portal* built on the front of the building.

The designs in *La Casa Adobe* emphasize territorial-style homes with an "open porch or bridge type portal forming one side of the patio" that would "let a breeze flow through the patio and keep it cool" during the summer.[12] Such designs center on the patio, with public and private rooms arranged around the central courtyard. A second series of drawings relies on the centralized hall layout and often includes a large living room at the end of the central hall.

Four years after the publication of *La Casa Adobe*, Lumpkins embarked on his Pueblo-based drawings. Although the designs were never built and were heretofore unpublished, they continue to raise provocative questions about the sources in modern residential architecture in the Southwest.

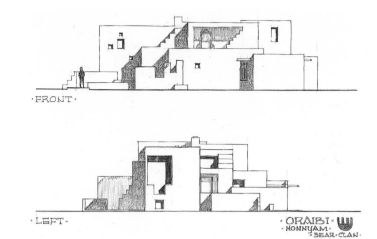

FIGURE 6.
William Lumpkins, *Bear Clan*, 1965–67, graphite on paper. Overhangs and large undercut windows cast shadows that accentuate the layering of facades and differentiate the roof heights.

DEFINING A MULTILEVEL
PUEBLO EXTERIOR

LUMPKINS POSES TWO questions that he answers throughout this project. First, he wonders how residences can be planned visually to reflect the appearance of historic Pueblo exteriors. Secondly, he investigates how residences can be planned internally to meet the needs of modern living while still maintaining the affective power of Pueblo architecture. In the course of his forty-eight designs, Lumpkins resolves the two issues by creating a dialectic between them.

The ancient and modern Pueblo villages that Cosmos and Victor Mindeleff visited in the late nineteenth century emphasized formal planning around centralized

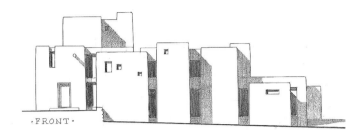

·FRONT·

FIGURE 7.
William Lumpkins, *Red Light of Dawn*, 1965–67, graphite on paper. Deep recesses separate the units of the residence and reinforce the vertical thrust of the two- and three-story room blocks. This conscious use of shadow-casting devices creates the illusion that the house is a series of added-on elements, not a single, unified structure.

public courtyards, asymmetrical planning within blocks of rooms, multistory construction with the use of rooftops as work spaces, randomly built additions, and solar principles applied to heating during winter and drying foodstuffs during summer.

Lumpkins began his development of Pueblo-based architecture by incorporating the look of multistory Pueblo room blocks into his designs. He based his investigation on Victor Mindeleff's views of the Hopi villages and of Zuni Pueblo with its related farming villages, translating the forms into simplified elevation renderings in order to distill via contour drawings and shadowing the essence of the architecture.[13]

Two general styles of Pueblo architecture are transformed into the designs. In the first he adapts the long, multistoried room blocks found in the larger residential units at Hopi and Zuni (plates 1, 5, and 6). A second style characterized by self-contained, multistory buildings comes from the smaller Hopi villages and the Zuni farming villages (plates 2 and 4).

Lumpkins uses split-level designs to compress three-story pueblos into a two-story private residences and still maintain the look of a massive pueblo buildings. By splitting levels, choosing uneven sites, and consciously placing slightly higher rooms toward the center of a building, the designer creates the illusion that two-story buildings are actually three-story units.

Lumpkins carefully formulates his designs to cast shadows that will articulate one section of a building from another and reinforce the appearance of multiple stories. Beginning with his first project, *Bear Clan* (figure 6, plate 1), he incorporates overhangs and large undercut windows to accentuate the layering of facades and differentiate roof heights. Similarly, the main facade of his second project, *On the Slope* (plate 2), includes narrow shadow-casting crevices that create the illusion of separate but connected units built as a series of added-on elements, common in Pueblo structures. The use of this device is most apparent in *Red Light of Dawn* (figure 7, plate 19) in which the deep recesses separate the units of the residence and simultaneously reinforce the vertical thrust of the two- and three-story room blocks.

To establish the appearance of a mud-plastered, stonemasonry Pueblo building, Lumpkins specifies adobe as the principal building material. Adobe is a natural material, is easily laid as straight or gently curved walls, can be sculpted as a plastic medium, and offers important heat-storage qualities for passive solar construction. Adobe resists inclement weather and rapid changes in temperature when properly sealed with stucco.

While adobe is a traditional building material in modern Pueblo villages along the Rio Grande Valley in New Mexico, stonemasonry was the preferred material used in most prehistoric Pueblo architecture throughout the Four Corners region. Often Lumpkins uses stonemasonry construction for circular structures adapted from ceremonial kivas in prehistoric floor plans. Lumpkins transforms these Pueblo spiritual centers into modern secular atriums for receiving guests or into living rooms with purely social functions. This concept of transformation is central to balancing the external look of and reference to Pueblo architecture with the needs of modern dwellers.

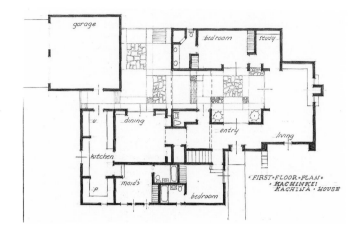

FIGURE 8.
William Lumpkins, *Kachina House*, 1965–67, graphite on paper. Flowing interior flagstone patios defined by "L" walls and glass partitions emphasize the openness of his public spaces and diminish the distinctions between the interior and exterior of the residence. The break with overly defined areas and functions develops into a major theme within this series of designs.

INTERIOR ARRANGEMENTS

LUMPKINS DEVELOPS THREE forms of interior organization from his Pueblo-based studies. In the first group, he organizes his houses along the division between public and private spaces popular in mainstream residential architecture. In an effort to understand Pueblo interior space, Lumpkins takes a radical turn in the second group by basing his designs on floor plans borrowed directly from prehistoric Pueblo ruins, many of them evincing wildly asymmetrical design-by-accretion. Finally, Lumpkins organizes a third group of dwellings on formal, balanced layouts based on symmetrical prehistoric floor plans. These formal layouts strongly resemble the formal organizational principles found in Lumpkins's earlier Spanish-Pueblo buildings.

To emphasize the distinction between public and private areas, Lumpkins often creates an entranceway that leads into a cluster of high-ceiling public rooms, which he segregates from a two-story wing of private rooms. He splits levels to help integrate the high-ceiling public rooms with the two-story private rooms. Bedrooms can be reached by walking up, or down, a short flight of stairs in this split-level

FIGURE 9.
Ground Plan of the Upper Part of Casa Blanca Ruin, figure 15 in Cosmos Mindeleff''s "The Cliff Ruins of Canyon de Chelly, Arizona." This prehistoric floor plan clarifies the concept of expansion through accretion and the absence of right angles within the building. This floor plan served as the model for the internal relationships in *Water Grass Place* (plate 27).

arrangement. Concealing the stairs to the upper floors reinforces the distinctions between public and private wings.

Within the first few designs Lumpkins abandons predictable interior relationships in favor of strongly asymmetrical designs. Rectilinear living and dining rooms combine to create a public sector that appears as a single great room. Glass dividers, masonry partitions, and L-shaped walls define the public spaces while maintaining an open structure within these residences. As the structure becomes less differentiated and more asymmetrically organized, functional designations become less specific. In time the dining room evolves into a functional area within a flowing public space rather than an area enclosed with walls.

This evolution can be understood by comparing the traditional rectilinear dining and living rooms in *Bear Clan* (plate 1) with the area of flowing patios defined by L-walls and glass windows in his third project, *Kachina House* (figure 8, plate 3), that serve as the dining and living rooms. By incorporating flagstone patios into these interior spaces, Lumpkins uses this material to push the openness of his public spaces and to signal the difficulty of distinguishing between the interior and exterior of the residence. The break with overly defined areas and functions develops into a major theme within this series of designs.

Beginning with his eighth project, Lumpkins initiates his experiments with layouts based on prehistoric Anasazi floor plans. His design for *Planting Moon* (plate 10) is based upon *Ground Plan of a Ruin on the Bottom Land in Canyon del Muerto* from Mindeleff's "Cliff Ruins," a prehistoric dwelling that shows strong evidence of growth by the accretion of new rooms. The modern dwelling developed from this layout is boldly asymmetrical in its maintenance of randomness from the Anasazi source. Similarly, *Water Grass Place* (figure 10, plate 27) emphasizes the sculptural use of adobe, the integration of flagstone pathways and portals, and the absence of right angles as found in the source ruins.

The use of Anasazi layouts turns toward the symmetrical in *Circle* (figure 11, plate 28), also derived from the Mindeleff study. In this project Lumpkins consciously chose a floor plan composed of rectilinear rooms surrounding a circular kiva. This ruin demonstrates planning rather than randomness in construction. The resulting residence transforms the circular kiva into a central open courtyard and entrance way. The use of altered kiva spaces as central structures of these residences strongly resembles the open courtyards and interior portals that dominate Lumpkins's Spanish-Pueblo designs beginning in the 1930s.

Circle initiates a series of projects that transforms kiva forms into courtyards, atriums (plate 34), and living rooms (plate 30). The use of transformed Anasazi floor plans intrigues Lumpkins, who works back and forth between planned and unplanned sources. The formal and asymmetric residences that result create the organizational opposites of a dialectic that strongly influences the interior divisions and exterior forms of Lumpkins's Pueblo-based residences.

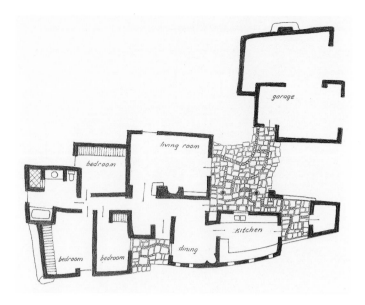

FIGURE 10.
William Lumpkins, *Water Grass Place*, 1965–67, graphite on paper. In this project Lumpkins emphasizes asymmetrical organization through the absence of right angles, the sculptural use of adobe, and the integration of flagstone pathways and portals into the residence.

SIGNS OF PUEBLO-NESS

INTERIOR DETAILS PLAY an important role in the definition of Lumpkins's adaption of Pueblo architecture to the needs of modern living. Ceilings, fireplaces, doors, windows, frescos, and solar heating details carefully affirm subtle differences with his Spanish-Pueblo architecture. Lumpkins's careful notation of his sources in the Mindeleffs' reports ascribes a kind of Pueblo "authenticity" to his designs.

Ceiling designs offer Lumpkins an opportunity to use strong graphic patterns to complement his organic use of plastered adobe and stonemasonry. Repeatedly he presents "reflected" ceilings to suggest ways of creating a sound roof structure on top of the eclectic placement of adobe walls. Visually Lumpkins relies heavily on the grid of vigas and the herringbone patterns created by the smaller latillas to unify his projects. Intellectually, these ceiling systems refer directly to prehistoric Anasazi ruins, historic Pueblo architecture, and to the exposed wooden structures associated with Arts and Crafts architecture. The asymmetrical floor plans, use of nonrectilinear rooms, and incomplete partition walls make the use of vigas and latillas a difficult and expensive roofing structure to build.

Lumpkins designs his public spaces around large, ceremonial fireplaces, less functional as efficient heat sources than symbolic of warmth of family. The presentations of fireplaces in Lumpkins's drawings issue from his study of Hopi and Zuni

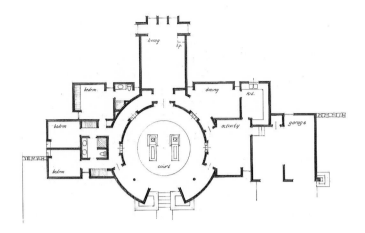

FIGURE II.
William Lumpkins, *Circle*,
1965–67, graphite on paper.
Lumpkins based *Circle* on a symmetrical prehistoric floor plan
composed of rectilinear rooms
surrounding a circular religious
chamber, or *kiva*. Lumpkins
transforms the religious structure
into the focus of the residence:
a central open courtyard and
entranceway. Such use of altered
kiva spaces strongly resembles the
open courtyards and interior
portals that dominate Lumpkins's
Spanish-Pueblo designs.

fireplaces in Victor Mindeleff's book. Early-twentieth-century Craftsman Style designs relied on the symbolic value of the fireplace. Fireplaces symbolized the core of Gustav Stickley's nostalgic ideal and were included in each of his designs for psy-chological as well as physical reasons. Stickley commented that "the hearthstone is always the center of true home life, and the very spirit of home seems to be lack-ing when a register or radiator tries ineffectually to take the place of a glowing grate or crackling leaping fire of logs."[14]

Lumpkins often repeats door shapes and fireplace details as window treatments. He uses a large T-shaped door form as a massive picture window in the living room of *Bear Clan* (plate 1), *On the Slope* (plate 2), and *Corn House* (plate 47). This shape refers to the T-shaped doors commonly found in the prehistorical Mesa Verde area and less commonly in nineteenth-century Hopi residences. Similarly, Lumpkins incorporates the chimney hoods from Hopi and Zuni pueblos as decorative treat-ments to shield the windows in projects such as *Yellow Light of Dawn* (plate 21). He also combines a T-shape window and chimneylike overhang in the master bedroom of *Greeting the Sun* (plate 25). The repetition of these forms creates visual relation-ships that unify several categories of architectural details within a single project.

Doors provide Lumpkins with yet another opportunity to integrate Pueblo-based designs and patterns into his conceptual projects. The composite sheet of door designs (plate 46) amplify the including of individual door designs through-out this series of drawings. The incorporation of handmade doors within these projects provides unifying graphic elements throughout each design. In addition to Pueblo references, these door designs consciously allude to the Arts and Crafts movement's use of handmade doors and hardware as symbols of security, thrift, and self-reliance.

Ironically, these Pueblo-based projects minimize the use of passive and active solar energy systems. Solar energy gain is sometimes associated with the large glass windows found in the living rooms of these residences. Active solar systems associ-ated with hot water solar collectors are included on the roofs of many projects. However, these structural systems are not visually part of his designs but are hidden behind parapet walls on the roof.

Lumpkins's documentation of Pueblo sources stands in stark contrast to the hybrid of Hispanic designs and generic Pueblo forms that were synthesized into the Pueblo Revival style early in the twentieth century. The repetition of these documented Pueblo details helps to unify a variety of exterior facades and interior arrangements. Taken as a whole, these details serve as signs of Pueblo-ness and accuracy within these modern adaptations of native architectural ideas.

· PLATES ·

FORTY-EIGHT RESIDENTIAL DESIGNS

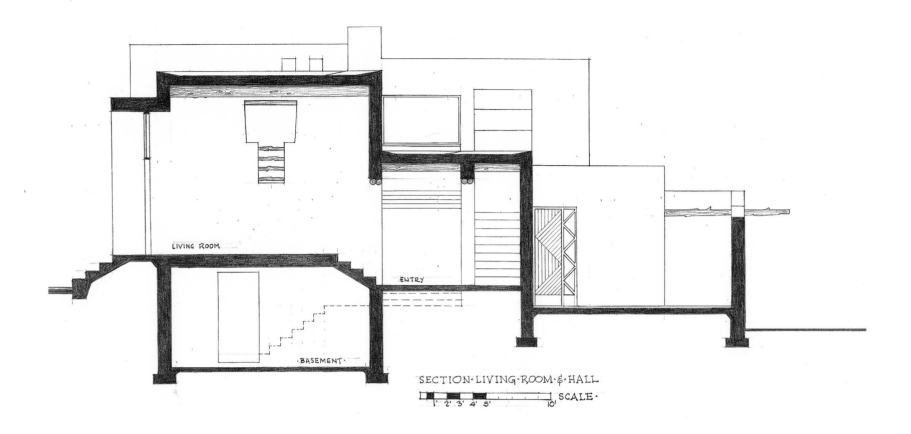

LIVING ROOM

ENTRY

·BASEMENT·

SECTION·LIVING·ROOM·&·HALL

·SCALE·

1' 2' 3' 4' 5'　　　10'

BEAR·CLAN·

PLATE 1. *Bear Clan*

Lumpkins employs shadows to define the exterior of his two-story design *Bear Clan*. A series of terraced patios leads visitors to the house and reinforces the multiple levels of the residence.[15] Internally Lumpkins repeats this landscaping feature through the inclusion of half-story divisions within the first floor. Structurally the design focuses on the dining area and adjoining exterior patios that he segregates from the private areas of the design.

The fenestration resembles the asymmetrical placement and size of the windows from the facade of the Hopi village Oraibi in eastern Arizona. The T-shaped door—commonly found in prehistoric Pueblo architecture from the Mesa Verde region of Colorado—specifies the shape of the window in the living room and serves as an important form dominating the exterior of the residence.

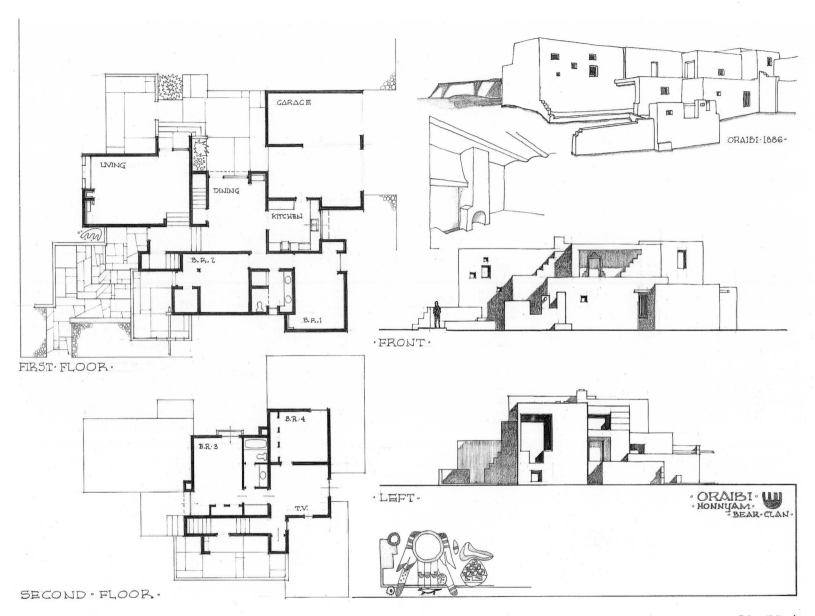

FIRST·FLOOR·

SECOND·FLOOR·

GARAGE

LIVING

DINING

KITCHEN

B.R. 2

B.R. 1

B.R. 3

B.R. 4

T.V.

ORAIBI·1886·

·FRONT·

·LEFT·

ORAIBI
·HONNYAM·
·BEAR·CLAN·

·PLATE·1·

PLATE I

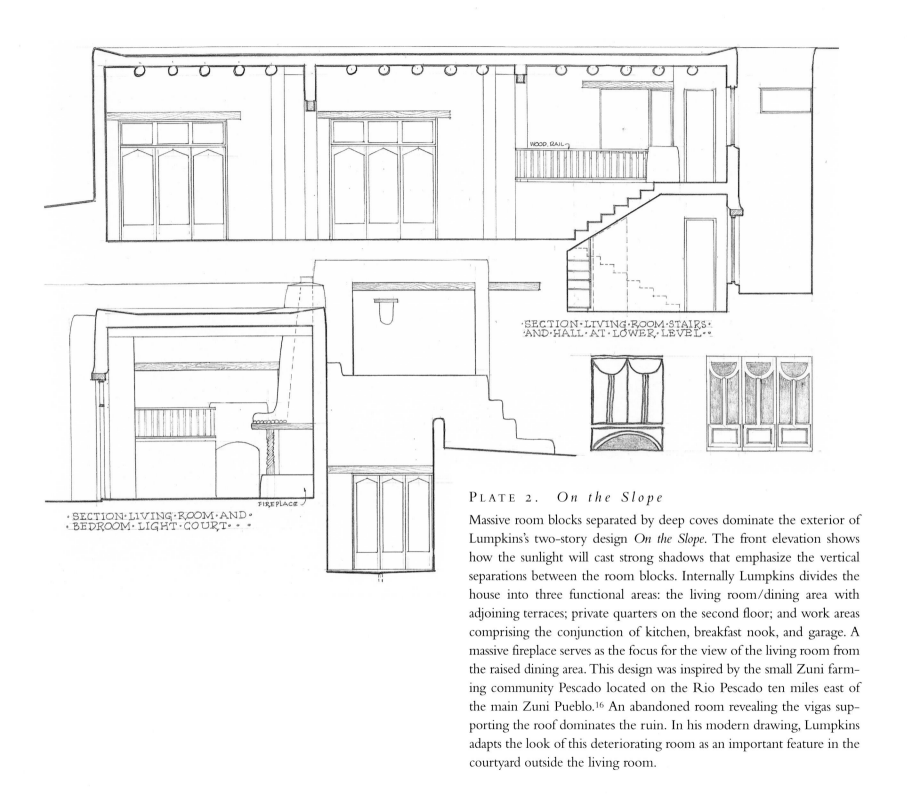

·SECTION·LIVING·ROOM·STAIRS·
·AND·HALL·AT·LOWER·LEVEL·

WOOD·RAIL

FIREPLACE

·SECTION·LIVING·ROOM·AND·
·BEDROOM·LIGHT·COURT·

PLATE 2. *On the Slope*

Massive room blocks separated by deep coves dominate the exterior of Lumpkins's two-story design *On the Slope*. The front elevation shows how the sunlight will cast strong shadows that emphasize the vertical separations between the room blocks. Internally Lumpkins divides the house into three functional areas: the living room/dining area with adjoining terraces; private quarters on the second floor; and work areas comprising the conjunction of kitchen, breakfast nook, and garage. A massive fireplace serves as the focus for the view of the living room from the raised dining area. This design was inspired by the small Zuni farming community Pescado located on the Rio Pescado ten miles east of the main Zuni Pueblo.[16] An abandoned room revealing the vigas supporting the roof dominates the ruin. In his modern drawing, Lumpkins adapts the look of this deteriorating room as an important feature in the courtyard outside the living room.

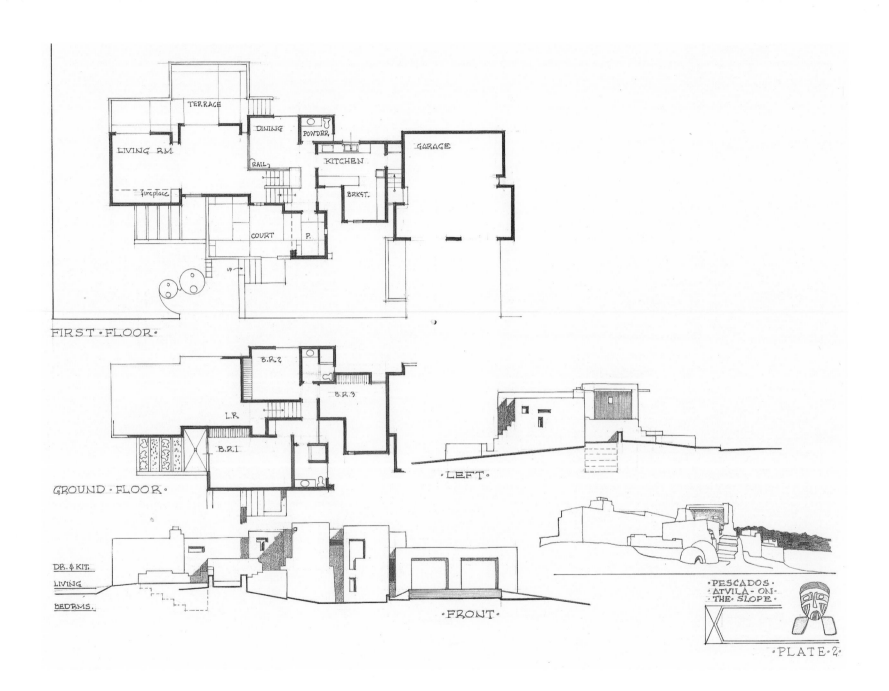

FIRST·FLOOR·

TERRACE

DINING

POWDER

LIVING·RM.

GARAGE

KITCHEN

RAIL

BRKST.

Fireplace

COURT

P.

UP

GROUND·FLOOR·

B.R.2

B.R.3

L.R.

B.R.1

·LEFT·

DR.&KIT.

LIVING

BEDRMS.

·FRONT·

·PESCADOS·
·ATVILA·ON·
THE·SLOPE·

·PLATE·2·

PLATE 2

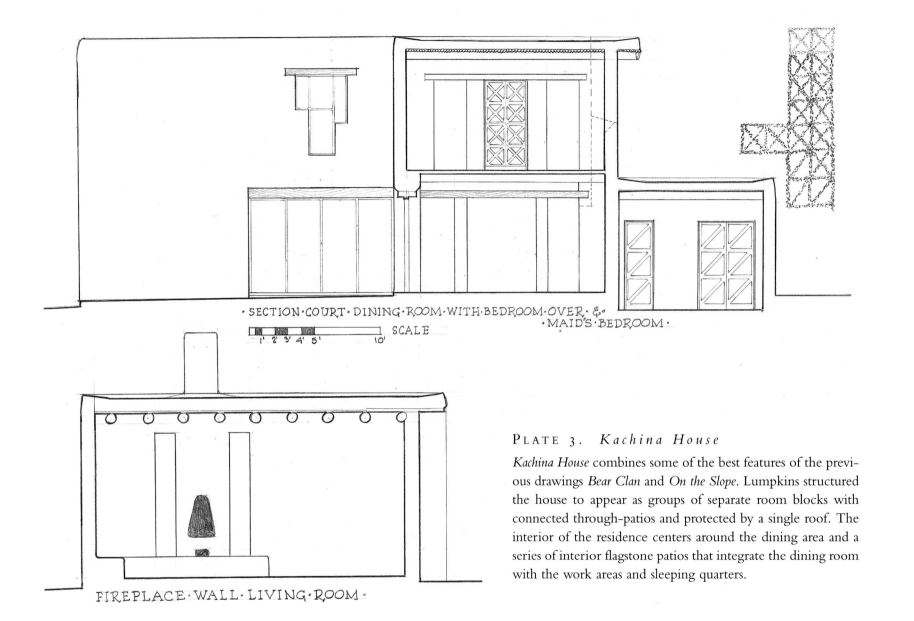

· SECTION · COURT · DINING · ROOM · WITH · BEDROOM · OVER · & ·
· MAID'S · BEDROOM ·

SCALE

1' 2' 3' 4' 5'   10'

· FIREPLACE · WALL · LIVING · ROOM ·

PLATE 3. *Kachina House*

Kachina House combines some of the best features of the previous drawings *Bear Clan* and *On the Slope*. Lumpkins structured the house to appear as groups of separate room blocks with connected through-patios and protected by a single roof. The interior of the residence centers around the dining area and a series of interior flagstone patios that integrate the dining room with the work areas and sleeping quarters.

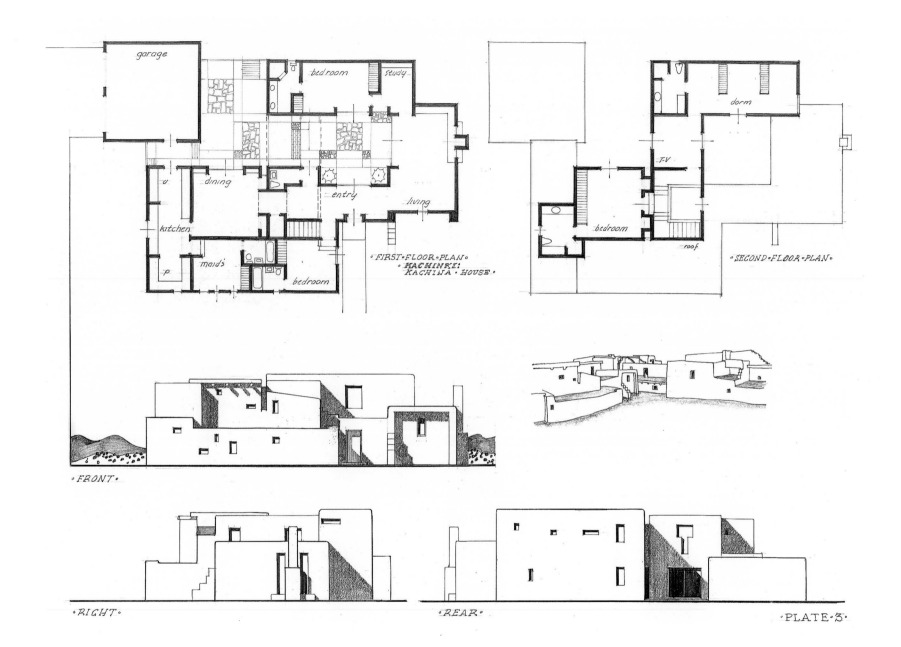

garage

bedroom   study

dining

kitchen   entry   living

maids

p   bedroom

·FIRST·FLOOR·PLAN·
·KACHINKI·
KACHINA·HOUSE·

dorm

T-V

bedroom

roof

·SECOND·FLOOR·PLAN·

·FRONT·

·RIGHT·   ·REAR·   ·PLATE·3·

PLATE 3

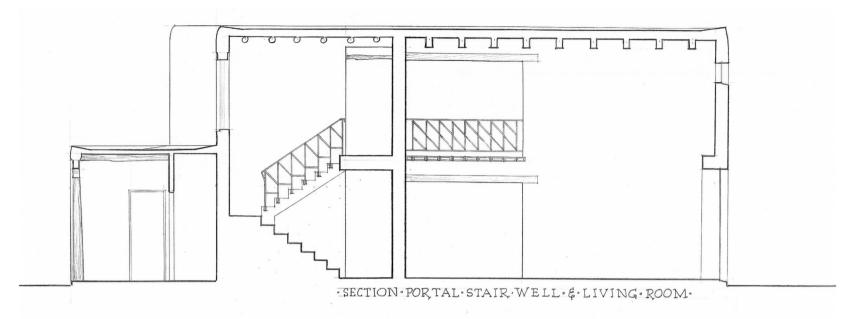

·SECTION·PORTAL·STAIR·WELL·&·LIVING·ROOM·

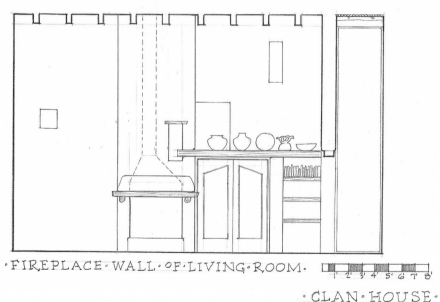

·FIREPLACE·WALL·OF·LIVING·ROOM·

·CLAN·HOUSE·

PLATE 4. *Clan House of Aholi*

The modern two-story design *Clan House of Aholi* relies on first-story rooms of differing heights to create the illusion of a larger, multistory pueblo.[17] Vertical separations between masses of adobe create the illusion of a building constructed through the addition of separate areas. Structurally the residence delineates between the public and private spaces. The public area centers on the two-stories-high living room, adjoining patios, a portal, and a massive fireplace with chimney. A large T-shaped window dominates the interior of the second-story studio and provides north light to the work space. Visually this high window balances the shadows cast by the first-floor portal on the northern exterior of the building.

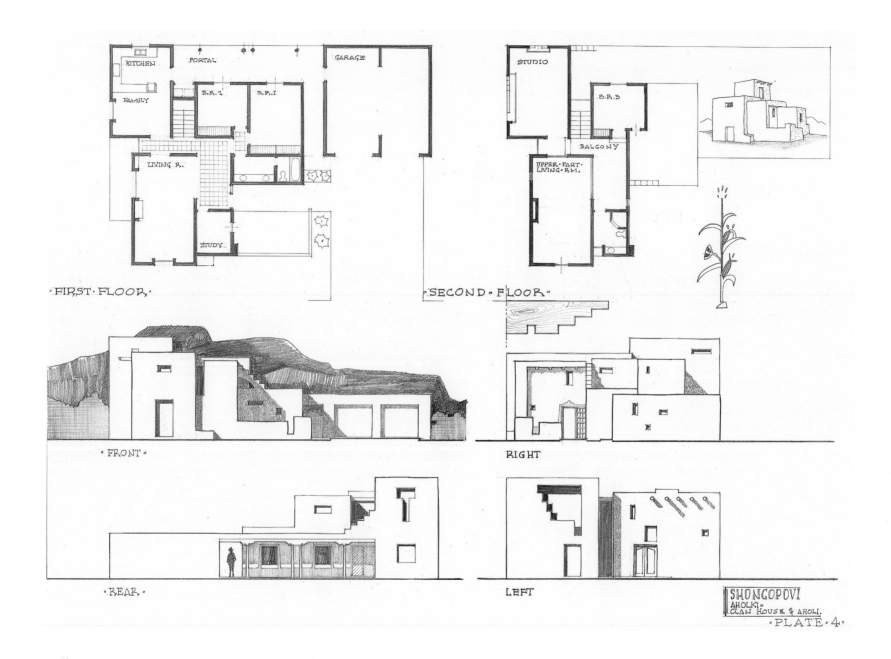

KITCHEN   PORTAL   GARAGE

FAMILY   B.R.2   B.R.1

LIVING R.

STUDY

·FIRST·FLOOR·

STUDIO   B.R.3

BALCONY

UPPER·PART·
LIVING·RM·

·SECOND·FLOOR·

·FRONT·

RIGHT

·REAR·

LEFT

SHONGOPOVI
AHOLKI·
CLAN HOUSE & AHOLI.
·PLATE·4·

PLATE 4

PLATE 5. *Eagle Land*

A large living room connected to walled court-yards forms the core of Lumpkins's drawing *Eagle Land*. Visually the two spaces function as a single meandering room within the residence although glass physically partitions the living room from the courtyards. The kitchen with dining area, the garage, and the single bedroom on the first floor seem like isolated units appended to the open space created by the living room and the courtyards. The bedrooms and study on the second floor are organized as a linear block of rooms, accented with partition walls and roofed overhangs as recorded at Zuni Pueblo in the nineteenth century.[18] The Zunis used deep overhangs to screen the sun during hot summers, an element that Lumpkins repeatedly uses as a major exterior element in his modern design *Eagle Land*.

EAGLE·LAND··KWÁVASA

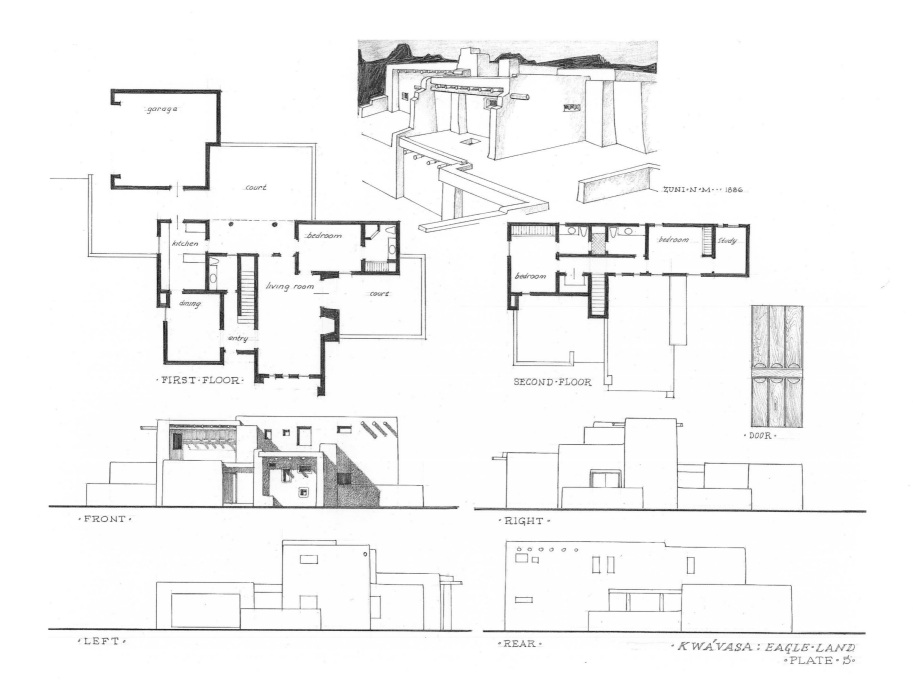

garage

court

kitchen

bedroom

living room

dining

court

entry

ZUNI·N·M···1886

FIRST·FLOOR

SECOND·FLOOR

bedroom

bedroom

study

·DOOR·

·FRONT·

·RIGHT·

·LEFT·

·REAR·

·KWÁ·VASA : EAGLE·LAND
·PLATE·5·

PLATE 5

PLATE 6. *Mishongovi*

Lumpkins further breaks with the symmetry of mainstream Western architecture in this residence based on an elevation view of the Hopi village Mishongovi.[19] The complete asymmetry of the floor plan dominates the design. Structurally, the plan isolates from the rest of the residence a private, two-story unit composed of bedrooms, baths, a study, and patios. This block of rooms serves as a backdrop for a high-ceiling, one-story public unit composed of a living room and courtyard separated by a portal. The chimney is an interior and exterior detail that alludes to the presence of the fireplace, the symbolic center of the residence. Here again, the kitchen and dining area mediate between the massive block of private spaces and the public living area.

· MISHONGOVI ·

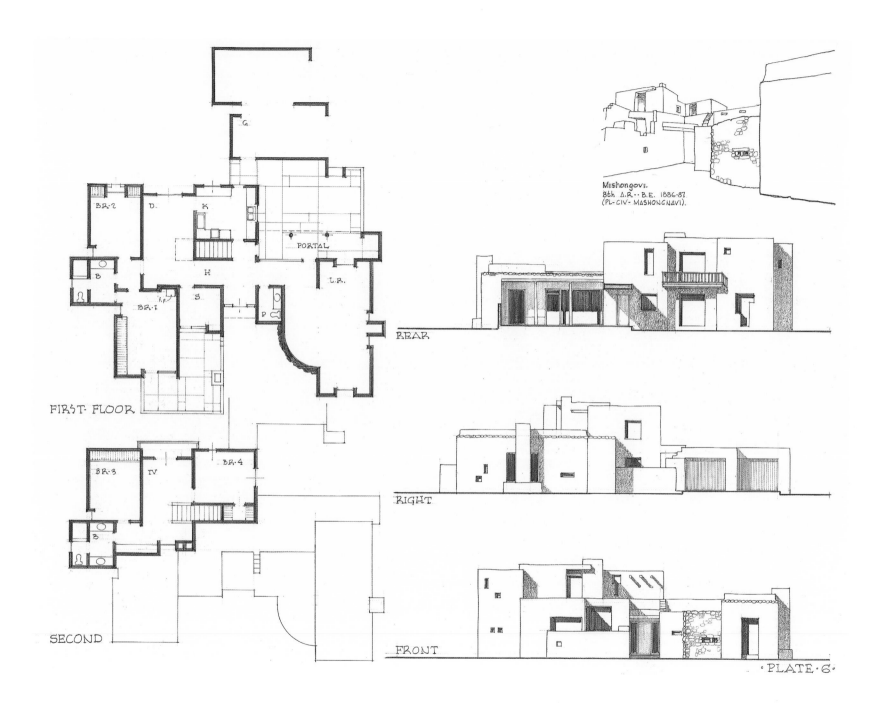

FIRST·FLOOR

SECOND

BR·2 D. K G

PORTAL

B H L.R.

BR·1 S P

BR·3 TV BR·4

B

Mishongovi.
8th A.R.--B.E. 1886-87
(PL·CIV·MASHONGNAVI).

REAR

RIGHT

FRONT

·PLATE·6·

PLATE 6

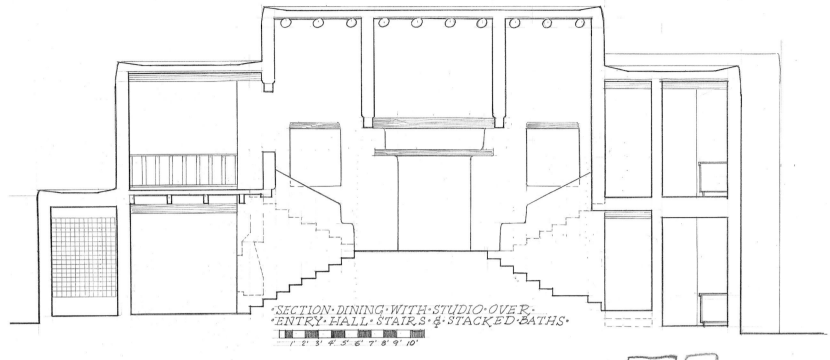

·SECTION·DINING·WITH·STUDIO·OVER·
·ENTRY·HALL·STAIRS·&·STACKED·BATHS·

1' 2' 3' 4' 5' 6' 7' 8' 9' 10'

·ANTELOPE·HOUSE·

PLATE 7. *Antelope House*

Romantic details dominate Lumpkins's design *Antelope House*. The study begins with a rendering of a complex fireplace from the Hopi village of Walpi, which Lumpkins incorporates into the corner of the library.[20] This design features the importance of romantic southwestern ideals, such as the symbiotic relationship between good books and a glowing piñon fire on a cold winter night. Lumpkins returns to a more symmetrical floor plan in *Antelope House*, which he organizes around a courtyard entrance, an entry hall, and living room. This cluster forms the central axis of the design, with private living spaces organized around this central pubic axis. The residence splits into multiple levels that offset the structural balance of the floor plan.

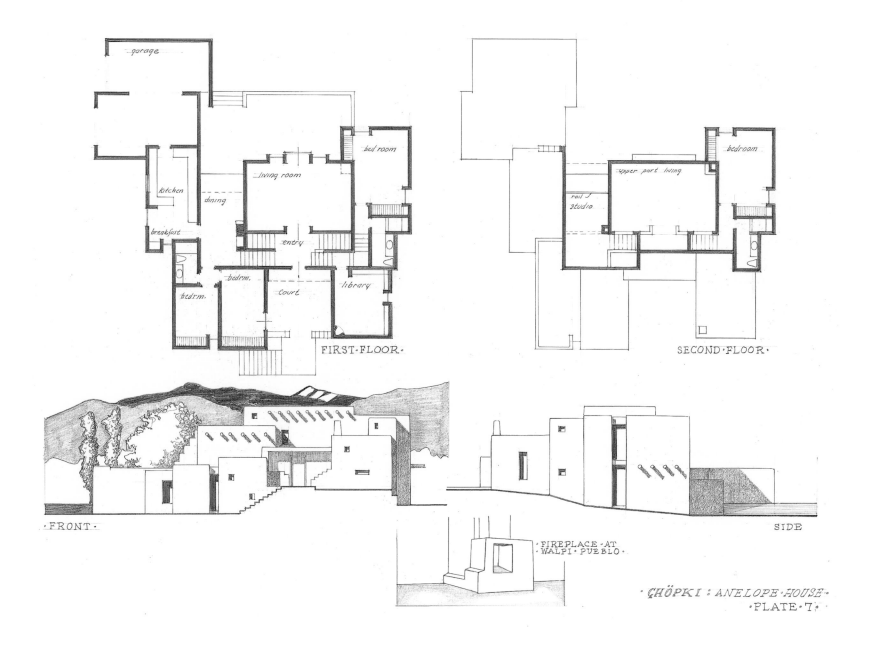

garage

kitchen

dining

breakfast

living room

bed room

bedrm.

bedrm.

court

entry

library

FIRST·FLOOR·

rail studio

upper part living

bedroom

SECOND·FLOOR·

FRONT·

FIREPLACE·AT
WALPI·PUEBLO·

SIDE

·ÇHÖPKI : ANELOPE·HOUSE·
·PLATE·7·

PLATE 7

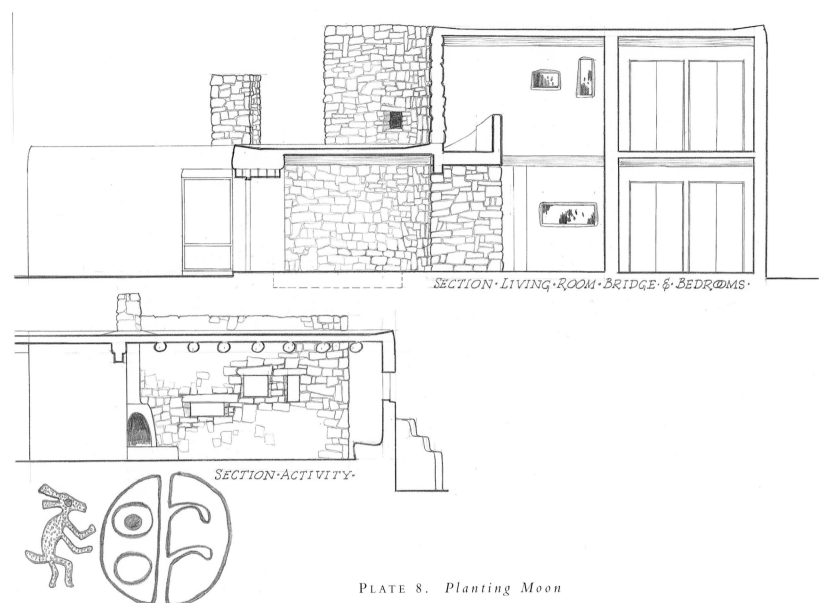

SECTION·LIVING·ROOM·BRIDGE·&·BEDROOMS·

SECTION·ACTIVITY·

PLATE 8. *Planting Moon*

Planting Moon shifts to a prehistoric architectural floor plan from Canyon de Chelly in eastern Arizona as source material.[21] The floor plan defines the relationship between a rectilinear block of habitation rooms and a subterranean kiva. In Lumpkins's reinterpretation the kiva rooms become intimate spaces that function as living rooms. By shifting his materials from smooth adobe to textured stonemasonry, Lumpkins focuses attention on the circular living room and thus encourages intimate social interaction.

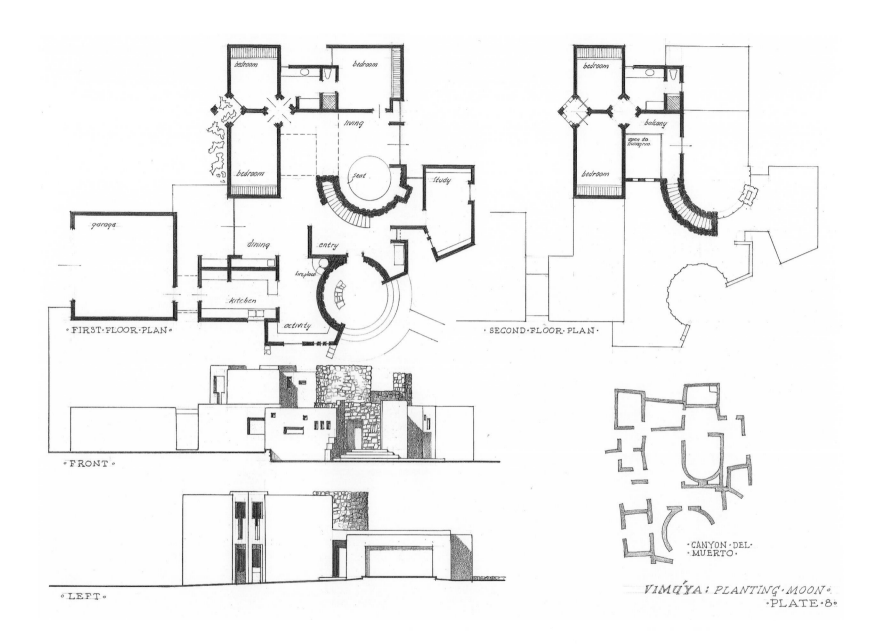

·FIRST·FLOOR·PLAN·

garage

bedroom

bedroom

living

bedroom

seat

study

dining

entry

fireplace

kitchen

activity

·SECOND·FLOOR·PLAN·

bedroom

balcony

open to livingrm.

bedroom

·FRONT·

·LEFT·

·CANYON·DEL· MUERTO·

VIMÚYA: PLANTING·MOON·
·PLATE·8·

PLATE 8

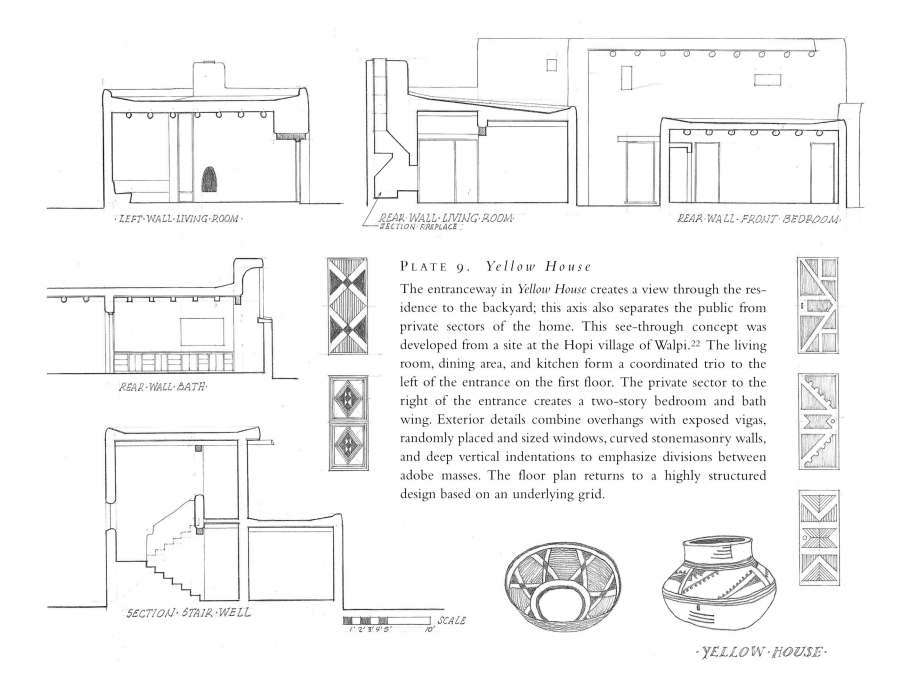

·LEFT·WALL·LIVING·ROOM·

·REAR·WALL·LIVING·ROOM·
·SECTION·FIREPLACE·

REAR·WALL·FRONT·BEDROOM·

·REAR·WALL·BATH·

SECTION·STAIR·WELL

SCALE
1' 2' 3' 4' 5'   10'

PLATE 9. *Yellow House*

The entranceway in *Yellow House* creates a view through the residence to the backyard; this axis also separates the public from private sectors of the home. This see-through concept was developed from a site at the Hopi village of Walpi.[22] The living room, dining area, and kitchen form a coordinated trio to the left of the entrance on the first floor. The private sector to the right of the entrance creates a two-story bedroom and bath wing. Exterior details combine overhangs with exposed vigas, randomly placed and sized windows, curved stonemasonry walls, and deep vertical indentations to emphasize divisions between adobe masses. The floor plan returns to a highly structured design based on an underlying grid.

·YELLOW·HOUSE·

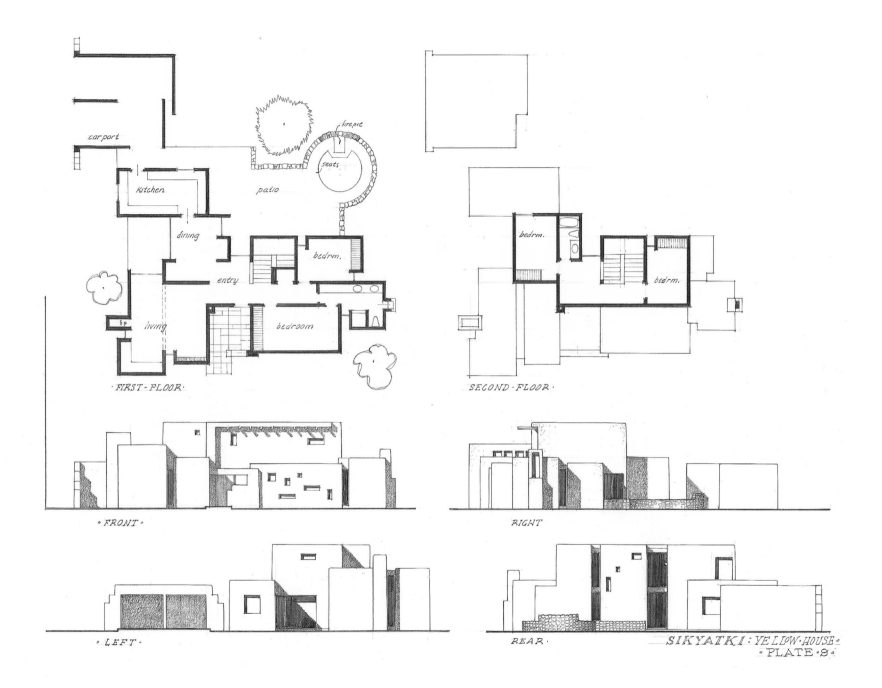

·FIRST·FLOOR·

carport

kitchen

dining

entry

living

fp

bedroom

patio

firepit

seats

bedrm.

·SECOND·FLOOR·

bedrm.

bedrm.

·FRONT·

·RIGHT·

·LEFT·

·REAR·

SIKYATKI : YELLOW·HOUSE·
·PLATE·9·

PLATE 9

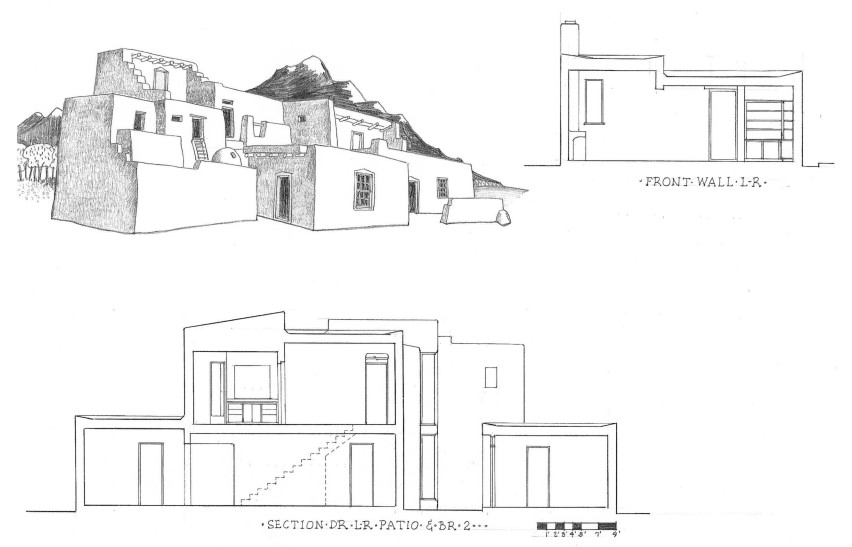

·FRONT·WALL·L·R·

·SECTION·DR·LR·PATIO·&·BR·2···

·JUNIPER·LEAVES·

PLATE 10. *Juniper Leaves*

Lumpkins again uses the fireplace as the symbolic center of a residential plan. He bases the design on the hooded fireplaces popular in Pueblo homes at the end of the nineteenth century. This version, based upon a Zuni Pueblo fireplace, is flanked by two narrow vertical windows.[23] The high chimney carries this detail to the exterior facade. A second rendition of the fireplace hood on the exterior of the second floor repeats the motif and also shields a pair of narrow, vertical windows. The exterior fractures into multiple units that affirm the look of nineteenth-century Pueblo structures.

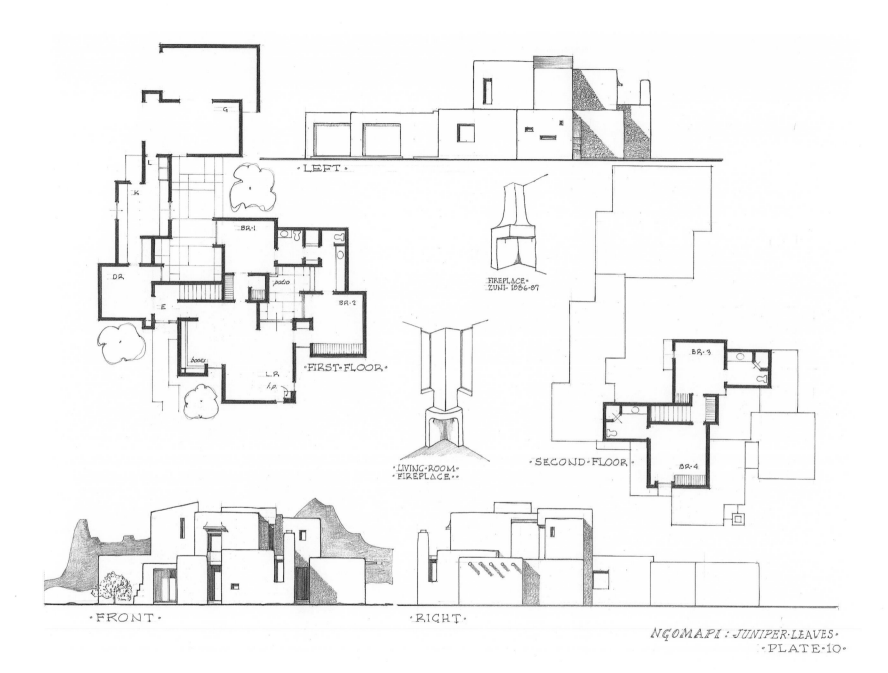

· LEFT ·

G

L

K

DR

E

BR·1

patio

BR·2

books

L.R.

f.p.

· FIRST·FLOOR ·

FIREPLACE·
ZUNI· 1886-87

· LIVING·ROOM·
·FIREPLACE·

BR·3

· SECOND·FLOOR ·

BR·4

· FRONT ·

· RIGHT ·

NGOMAPI : JUNIPER·LEAVES·
·PLATE·10·

PLATE 10

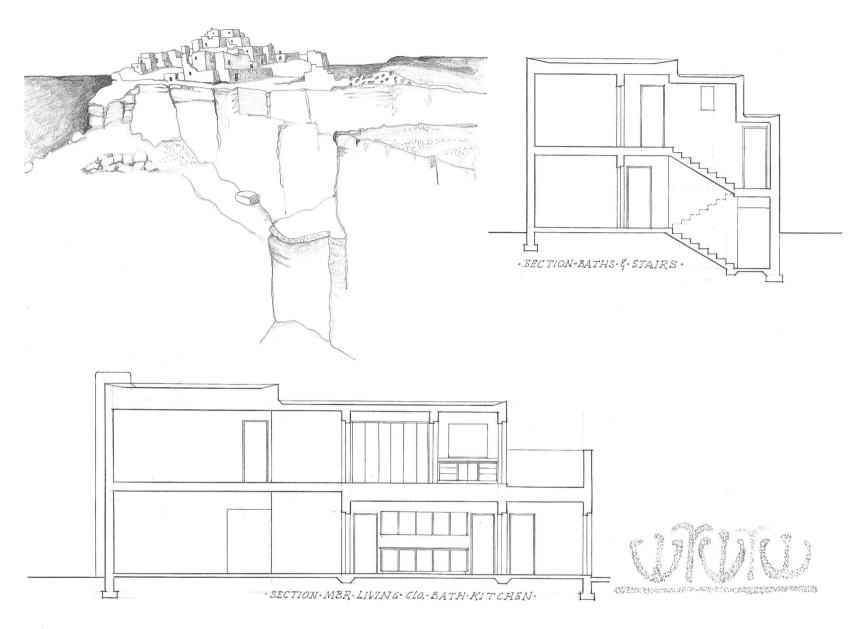

·SECTION·BATHS·&·STAIRS·

·SECTION·MBR·LIVING·CLO·BATH·KITCHEN·

PLATE II. *Sagebrush*

Lumpkins bases the exterior of his design *Sagebrush* on the facade of Walpi at Hopi First Mesa.[24] This village presents the classic view of multistory Pueblo architecture that mimics the natural geology of the surrounding landscape. In the Lumpkins plan, the front facade emphasizes multilevel, overlapping forms and deep recesses that create the look of nineteenth-century Pueblo architecture.

Internally this project combines the kitchen, breakfast nook, dining room, and living room into a logical area separated from the private rooms by a see-through entrance hall, again borrowing from Walpi's passageway design.

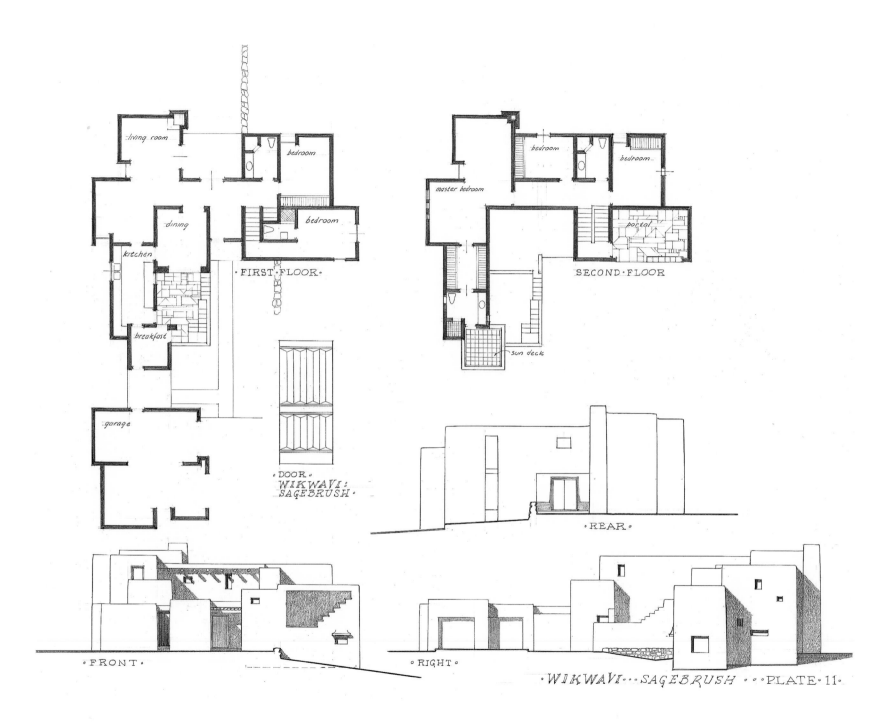

living room

bedroom

dining

bedroom

kitchen

·FIRST·FLOOR·

breakfast

garage

·DOOR·
WIKWAVI:
SAGEBRUSH·

bedroom

bedroom

master bedroom

portal

·SECOND·FLOOR·

sun deck

·REAR·

·FRONT·

·RIGHT·

·WIKWAVI···SAGEBRUSH···PLATE·11·

PLATE II

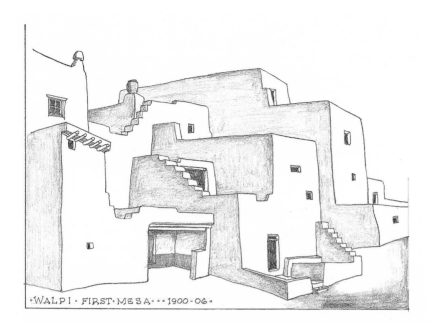

·WALPI · FIRST · MESA · · · 1900-06 ·

PLATE 12. *Twilight*

Lumpkins returns to the importance of fireplaces and doorways as details that symbolize and unify such complex projects as *Twilight*. His use of T-shaped doorways and a corner fireplace serves as examples of Pueblo-based icons that clarify the origins of this series of drawings.[25] *Twilight* is a complex two-story project that asymmetrically separates living room from the private aspects of the residence and also breaks the two-car garage into two individual units.

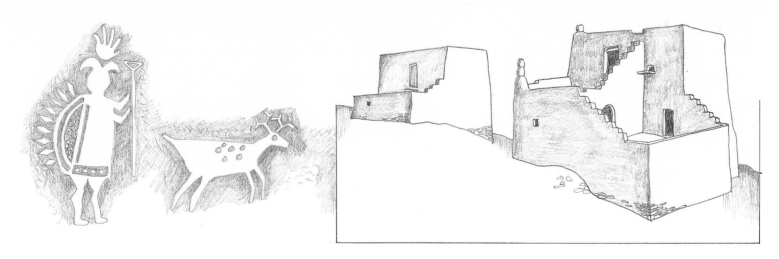

TA'SNPI

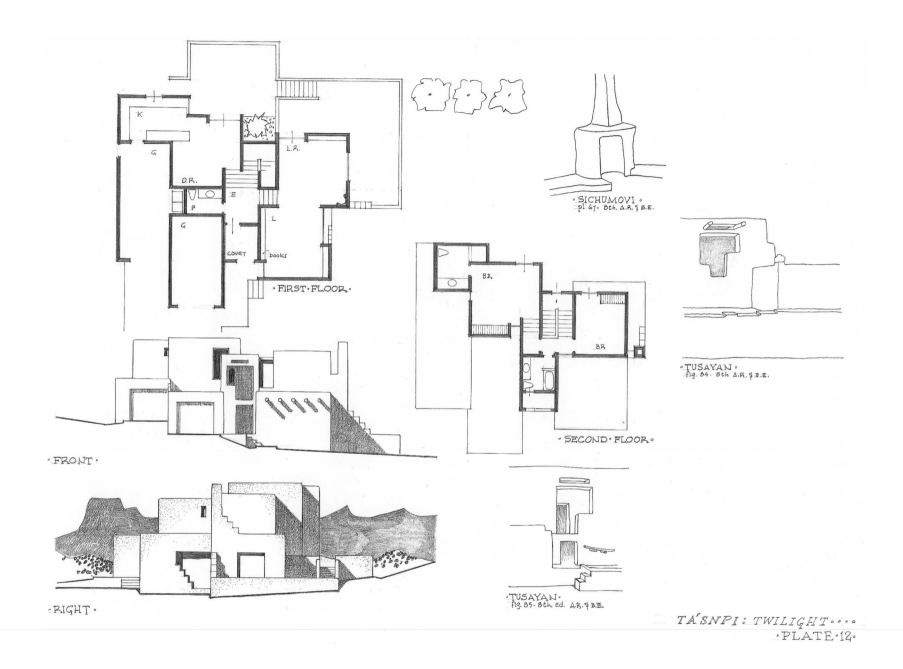

K

G

D.R.

E

P

G

L.R.

L

COURT

books

·FIRST·FLOOR·

·FRONT·

·RIGHT·

B.R.

B.R.

·SECOND·FLOOR·

·SICHUMOVI·
pl. 67 - 8th. A.R. & B.E.

·TUSAYAN·
fig. 64 - 8th A.R. & B.E.

·TUSAYAN·
fig. 65 - 8th. ed. A.R. & B.E.

TA'SNPI : TWILIGHT ···
·PLATE·12·

PLATE 12

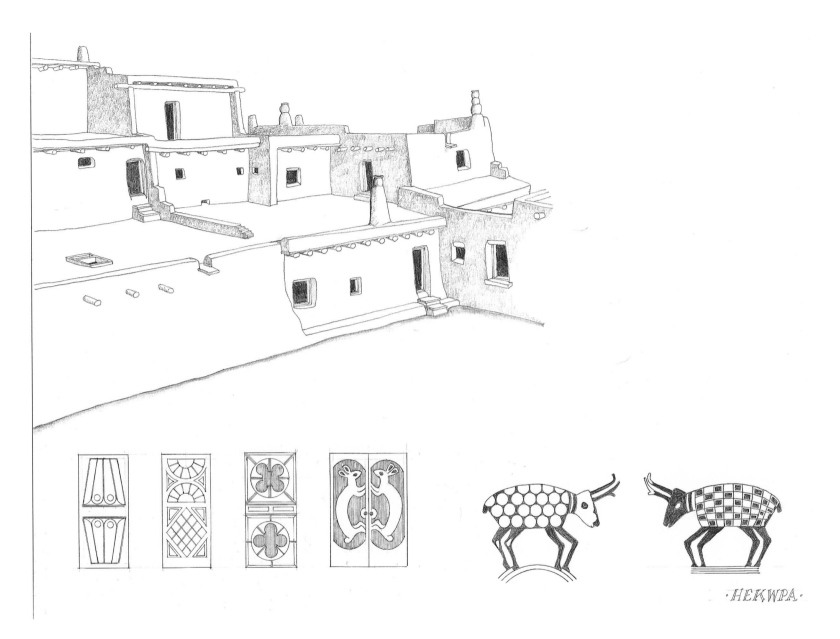

·HEKWPA·

PLATE 13. *Oak Tree*

Oak Tree presents a two-story residence with a connected one-story living room. The use of enclosed patios creates an open structure that segregates private rooms into separate units and psychologically negates the distinction between interior and exterior spaces. A corner fireplace, with a massive exterior chimney, dominates the public living room.

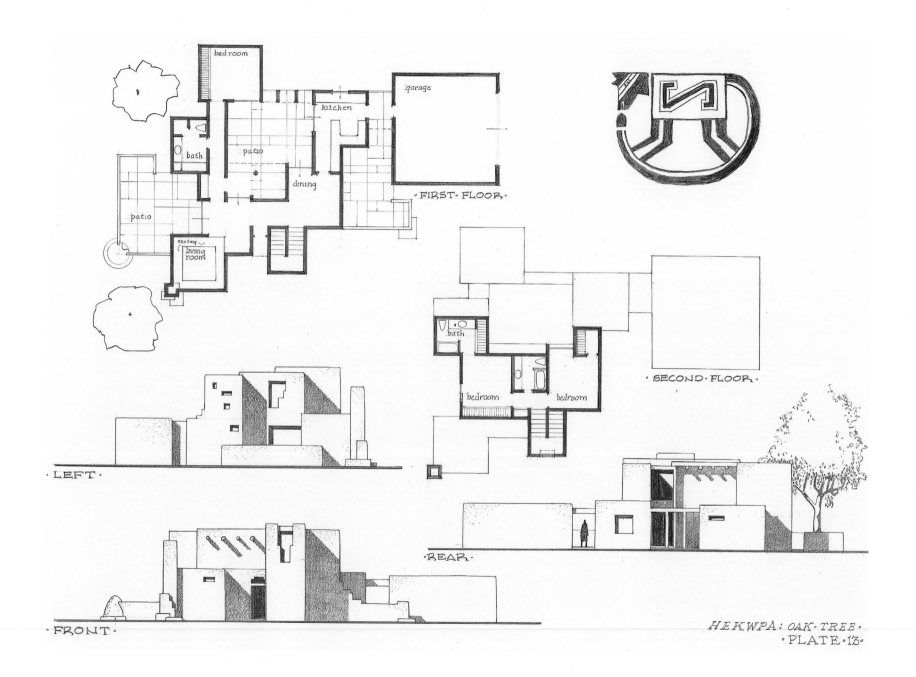

bedroom

garage

kitchen

bath

patio

dining

·FIRST·FLOOR·

patio

seating
living
room

bath

bedroom

bedroom

·SECOND·FLOOR·

·LEFT·

·REAR·

·FRONT·

HEKWPA: OAK·TREE·
·PLATE·13·

PLATE 13

PLATE 14. *Rock on High*

Rock on High creates a rambling, single- and two-story residence structured around a massive fireplace located in the living room. The single-story public spaces— entranceway, living room, library, gallery, and dining room—form one open, connected structure that Lumpkins carefully separates from the private two-story spaces. Asymmetric fenestration, parapets that carefully connect units, and the layering of sections against each other accentuate the mass of the building.

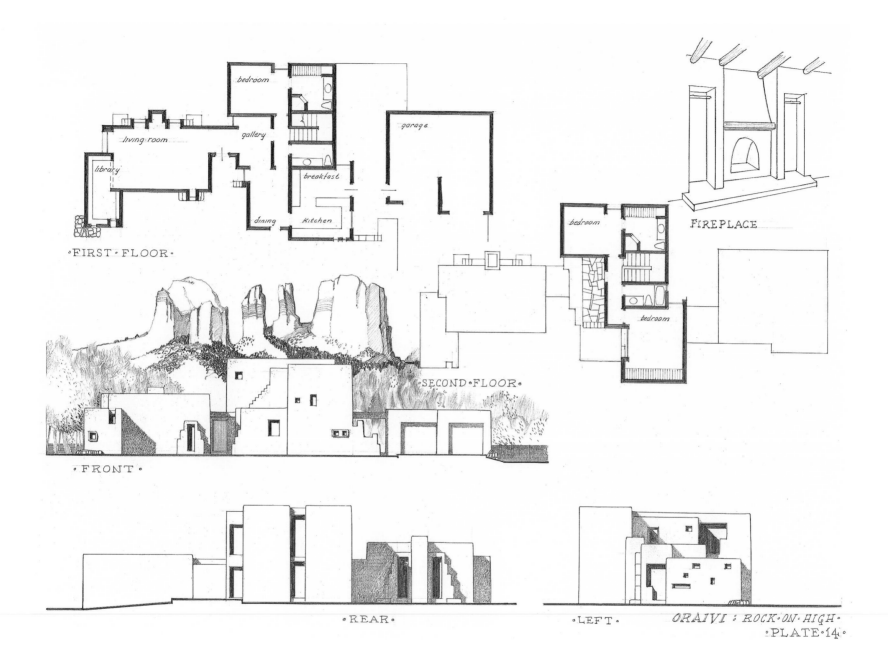

bedroom

living·room

gallery

library

garage

breakfast

dining

kitchen

·FIRST·FLOOR·

bedroom

FIREPLACE

·SECOND·FLOOR·

bedroom

·FRONT·

·REAR·

·LEFT·

ORAIVI : ROCK·ON·HIGH
·PLATE·14·

PLATE 14

PANGWUVI

PLATE 15. *Where the Bighorn Sheep Climb*

Where the Bighorn Sheep Climb segregates high-ceiling living and dining areas from both private areas (bedrooms and bathrooms) and kitchen. An open activity area leads outside through a portal and offers a transitional space between public and private areas. The massing of forms as the building moves from a single to a multistory residence is reminiscent of the structuring of Taos Pueblo in northern New Mexico.

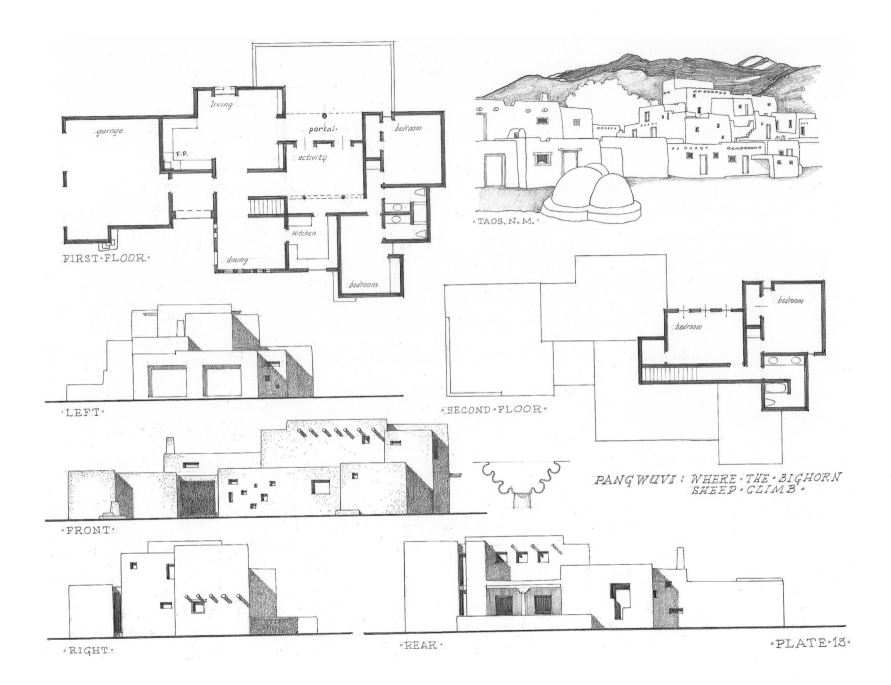

FIRST·FLOOR·

garage

living

portal

bedroom

F.P.

activity

kitchen

dining

bedroom

·TAOS. N. M.·

LEFT·

SECOND·FLOOR·

bedroom

bedroom

FRONT·

PANGWUVI : WHERE·THE·BIGHORN
SHEEP·CLIMB·

·RIGHT·

·REAR·

·PLATE·15·

PLATE 15

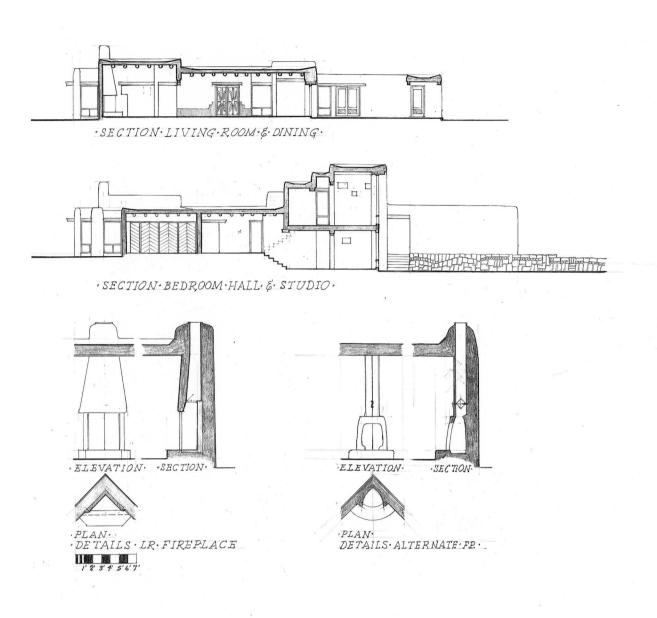

·SECTION·LIVING·ROOM·&·DINING·

·SECTION·BEDROOM·HALL·&·STUDIO·

·ELEVATION·   ·SECTION·

·PLAN·
·DETAILS·LR·FIREPLACE·

1'·2'·3'·4'·5'·6'·7'

·ELEVATION·   ·SECTION·

·PLAN·
·DETAILS·ALTERNATE·FP·

·PALA'TALA·

PLATE 16. *Sunrise*

The exterior of *Sunrise* asymmetrically organizes adobe forms of differing sizes to mimic nineteenth-century Pueblo architecture and the relationships between foothills and mountains. Internally Lumpkins organizes the project to use courtyards to separate public and private areas of the residence. The careful placement of glass walls repeatedly breaks the distinction between interior and exterior spaces. This project locates the kitchen away from the private activity areas of the studio and bedrooms.

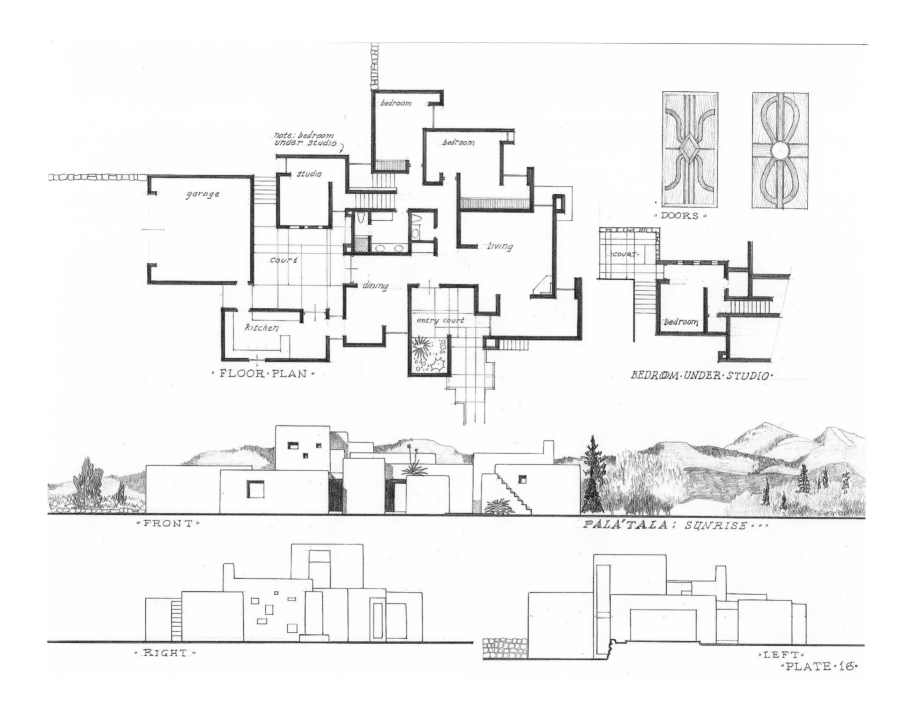

note: bedroom
under studio

studio

garage

court

dining

kitchen

bedroom

bedroom

living

entry court

· FLOOR · PLAN ·

· DOORS ·

court

bedroom

BEDROOM · UNDER · STUDIO ·

· FRONT ·

PALA'TALA : SUNRISE · · ·

· RIGHT ·

· LEFT ·
· PLATE · 16 ·

PLATE 16

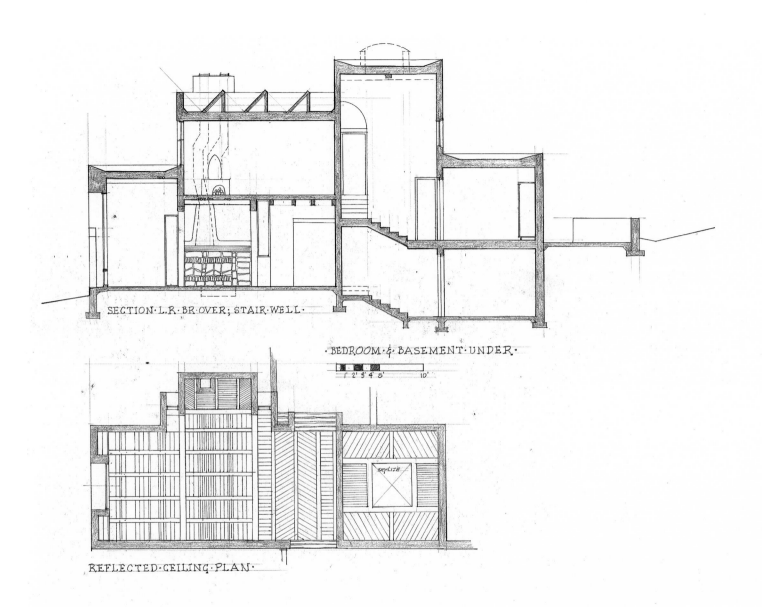

SECTION·L.R·BR·OVER; STAIR·WELL·

BEDROOM·&·BASEMENT·UNDER·

REFLECTED·CEILING·PLAN·

SKYLITE

PLATE 17. *Evergreen Village*

Evergreen uses door motifs as exterior motifs defining the fenestration of the facades. *Evergreen*[26] represents an asymmetrically organized residence with split two-car garages and public spaces separated from private ones. The reflected ceiling plan defines the difficulty of creating a roof structure for a split-level, open-structured dwelling.

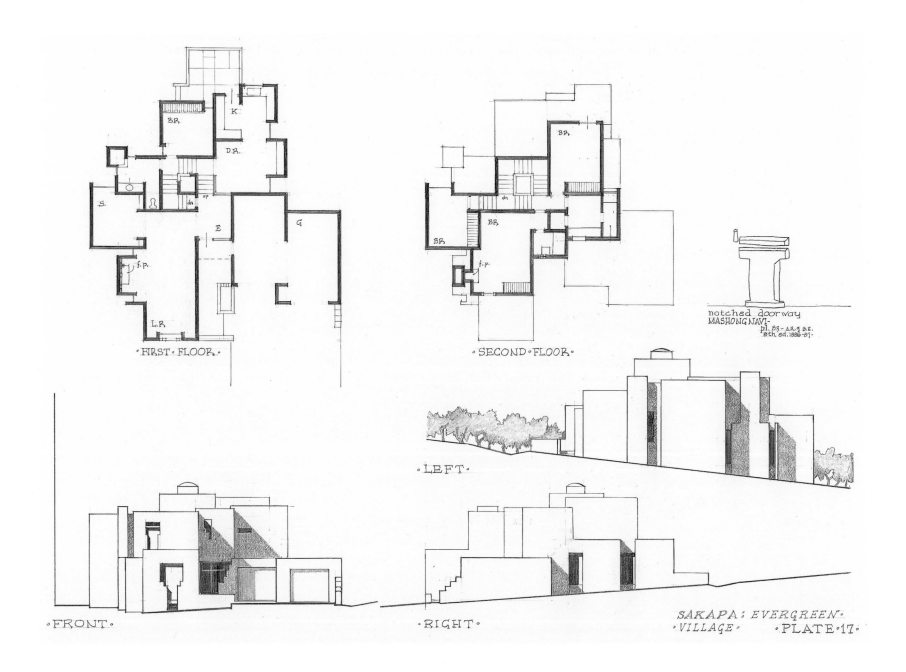

·FIRST·FLOOR·

BR
K
D.R.
S.
E
G
f.p.
L.R.

·SECOND·FLOOR·

BR
BR
BR
f.p.

notched doorway
MASHONG NAVI·
pl. 83 - A.R. q B.E.
8th. ed. 1886-87·

·LEFT·

·FRONT·

·RIGHT·

SAKAPA: EVERGREEN·
·VILLAGE·   ·PLATE·17·

PLATE 17

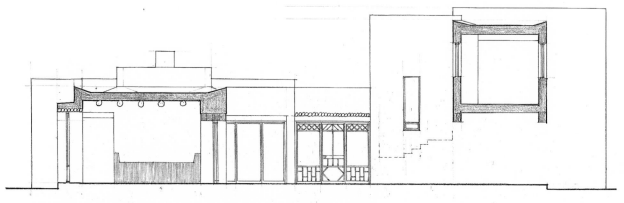

SECTION·DINING·PATIO·&·BRIDGE·2ND·FLOOR·BR·

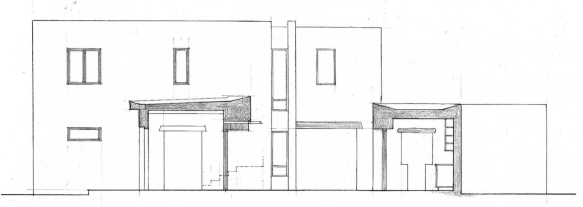

SECTION·ENTRY·PATIO·&·KITCHEN·

PLATE 18. *Water Planted Place*

Water Planted Place plays a two-story unit of private bedrooms, bathrooms, and a study against a unit combining the kitchen, dining area, and a high, single-story living room. The entranceway leads to an open patio that mediates between public and private spaces. The huge chimney, visible on the outside of the residence, provides a detail that alludes to the fireplace that dominates the living room. The formal relationship between the hearth and a built-in bookcase on each side directly repeats a popular Craftsman Style formula. Thin vertical windows set into the adobe face of *Water Planted Place* help to define the mass of the building by dividing the residence into more intimate units.

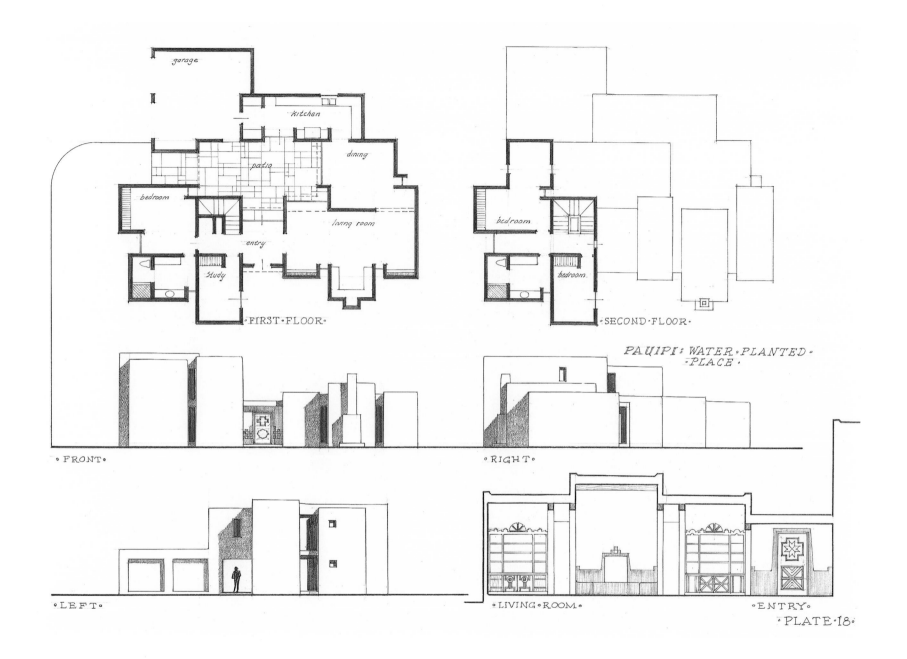

garage

Kitchen

dining

patio

bedroom

living room

entry

Study

·FIRST·FLOOR·

bedroom

bedroom

·SECOND·FLOOR·

PAUIPI: *WATER*·PLANTED·
·PLACE·

·FRONT·

·RIGHT·

·LEFT·

·LIVING·ROOM·

·ENTRY·
·PLATE·18·

PLATE 18

SECTION·ENTRY·LOOKING·AT·LR·DR·UP·TO·STUDY·HALL·MBR·OVER·&·EAST ·BEDROOM·

SECTION·LIVING·RM·STUDY·OVER·&·SOUTH· ·BEDROOMS·

·TALAWVA·

PLATE 19. *Red Light of Dawn*

Tall vertical windows set into recesses in the exterior walls of *Red Light of Dawn* provide light while the walls along the recesses simultaneously shield the interior from direct rays. Visually the recesses emphasize the vertical aspects of the project and define the massing of adobe forms. The entrance room and adjoining hallway separate the public from the private areas. The public areas are four steps above the hall level while the private rooms are six steps below the hallway. A two-sided fireplace with a single chimney separates the dining area from the living room.

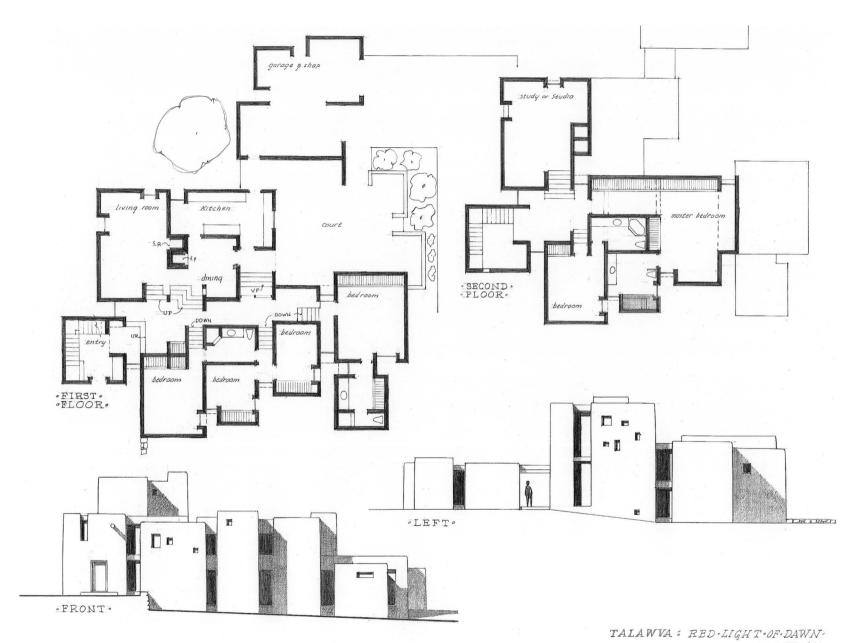

garage & shop

study or studio

living room   Kitchen

court

f.p.

f.p.

dining

master bedroom

UP

bedroom

UP

UP

DOWN

bedroom

SECOND
FLOOR

entry

DOWN

bedroom

bedroom

bedroom

bedroom

FIRST
FLOOR

LEFT

FRONT

TALAWVA : RED·LIGHT·OF·DAWN
· PLATE : 19 ·

PLATE 19

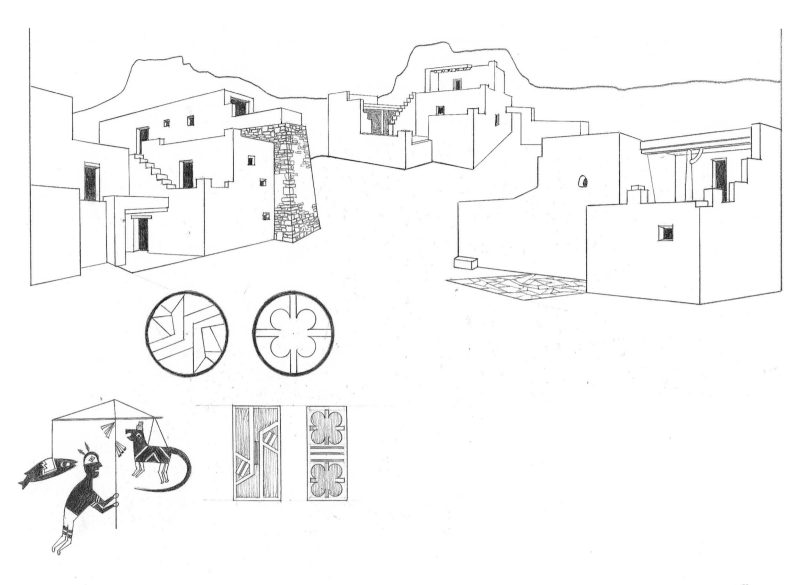

·MA'ÖVI·

PLATE 20. *Rabbit Brush (Chamisa)*

This asymmetrically organized residence centers around a monumental living room with an imposing fireplace and chimney. A glass wall on either side of the fireplace divides the interior of the living room from an exterior courtyard with trees and garden areas. The kitchen, dining room, and library cluster around the living room. Partly hidden by a partition, the entrance leads to a courtyard that separates the public spaces from the private bedrooms and from the access to additional bedrooms and bathrooms on the second floor.

Garage

kitchen

dining

bedroom

Court

living

library

Entry

bedroom

FIRST·FLOOR

bedroom

bedroom

SECOND
FLOOR

MA'ÖVI : RABBIT·BRUSH ·(CHAMISA)·
·PLATE·20·

PLATE 20

PLATE 21. *Yellow Light of Dawn*

Yellow Light of Dawn uses adobe as a sculptural medium to define the flowing exterior form and interior living areas of this residence. A partition wall with an open gate partially hides the entrance vestibule that leads to the public and private areas of the residence. Lumpkins groups the living room, kitchen, and dining room as one part of the house and creates a cluster of private rooms on the first floor and a second cluster of the upper floor. Low exterior walls define a series of courtyards that connect to the building through high portals with post-and-beam construction.

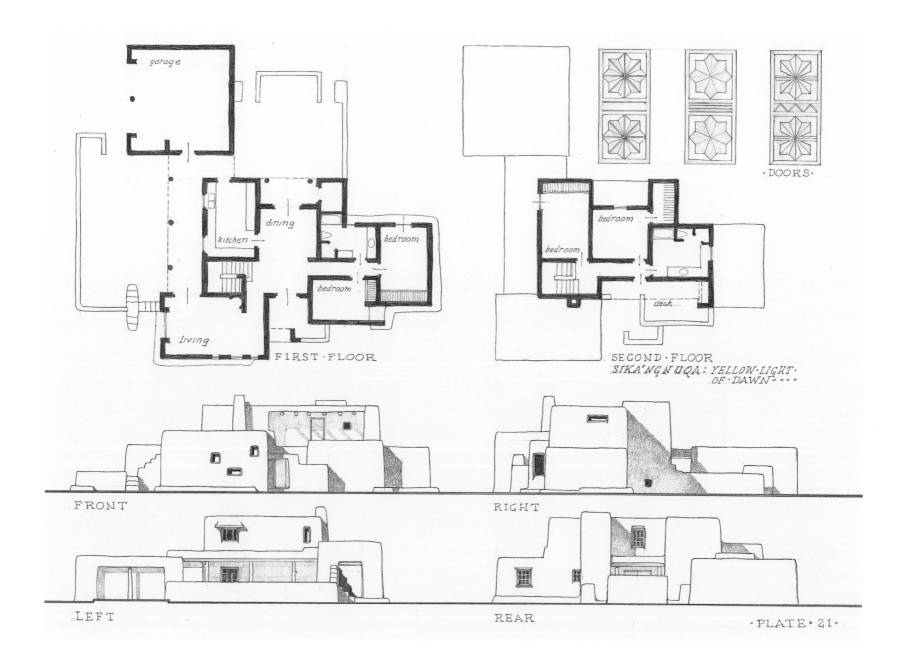

garage

dining

kitchen

bedroom

bedroom

living

FIRST · FLOOR

bedroom

bedroom

deck

SECOND · FLOOR

SIKA'NQNUQA : YELLOW · LIGHT · OF · DAWN · · · ·

· DOORS ·

FRONT

RIGHT

LEFT

REAR

· PLATE · 21 ·

PLATE 21

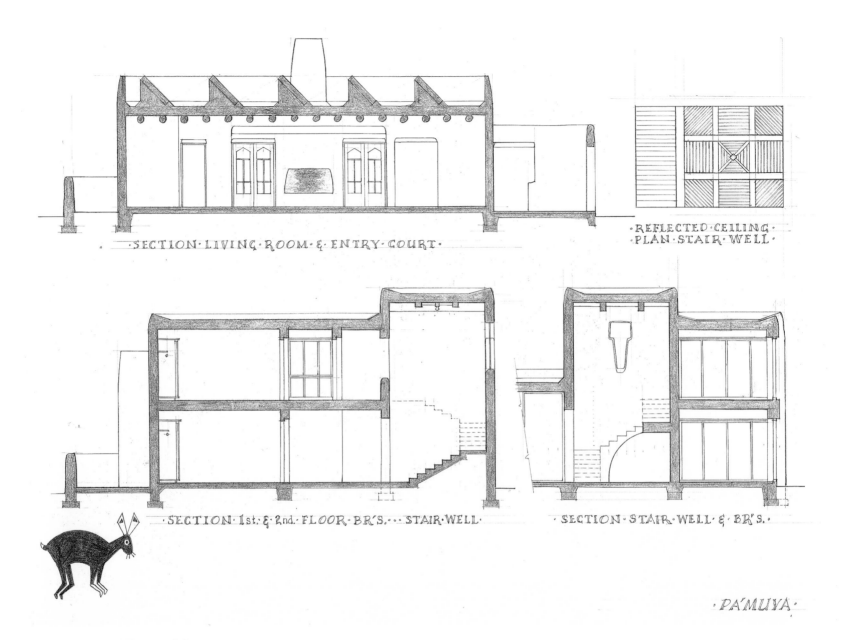

SECTION · LIVING · ROOM · & · ENTRY · COURT ·

· REFLECTED · CEILING ·
PLAN · STAIR · WELL ·

· SECTION · 1st. · & · 2nd. · FLOOR · BR'S. · · · STAIR · WELL ·

· SECTION · STAIR · WELL · & · BR'S. ·

· PA'MUYA ·

PLATE 22. *Water Moon*

Lumpkins designed *Water Moon* as an asymmetrical project that pairs blocks of rooms with exterior flagstone patios that are partially enclosed with low walls. A large entrance separates the private bedroom section from the public area of the house. The high ceiling of the living room is almost as high as the two-story bedroom unit. A massive fireplace with an exposed chimney forms the detail that connects the kitchen and library to the living room. Glass partitions connect room blocks, unify the project, and prevent the adobe walls of the residence from becoming visually overwhelming.

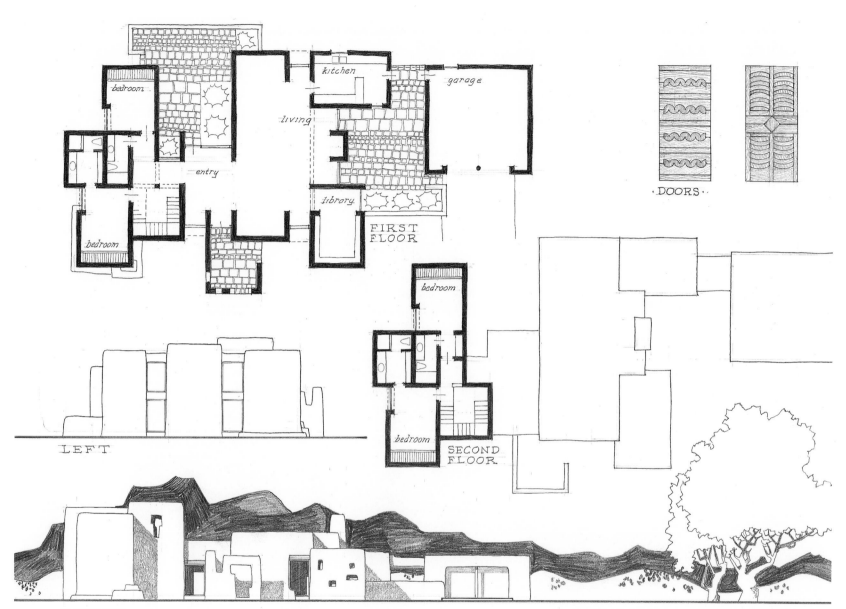

bedroom

kitchen

garage

living

entry

library

FIRST
FLOOR

bedroom

DOORS

bedroom

LEFT

bedroom

SECOND
FLOOR

FRONT

PÁMUYA: WATER·MOON···   ·PLATE·22·

PLATE 22

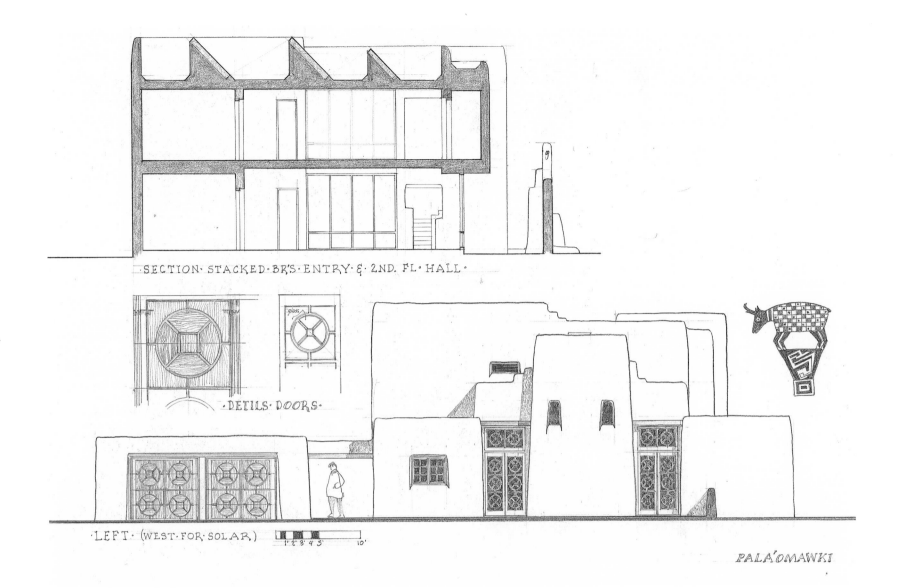

SECTION·STACKED·BR'S·ENTRY·&·2ND.·FL·HALL·

·DETILS·DOORS·

glass

·LEFT·(WEST·FOR·SOLAR·)

1' 2' 3' 4' 5'   10'

PALA'OMAWKI

PLATE 23. *Red House*

Red House breaks with the rectilinear use of adobe as a building material. This project begins to emphasize the imprecision of handmade materials to impart a crafted, owner-built quality to the residence. This project is asymmetrically organized with details such as integrated patios, irregular fenestration, and the massing of undulating forms appropriated from late-nineteenth-century Pueblo architecture.

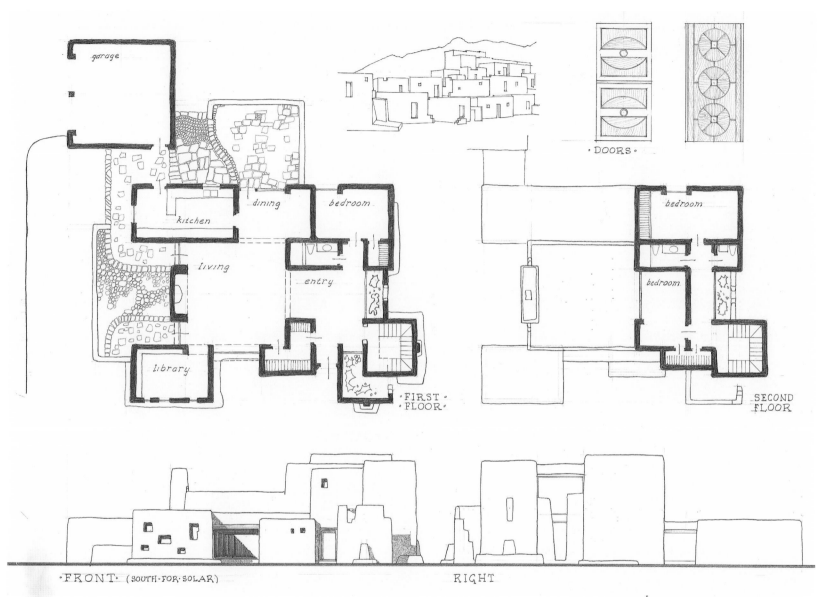

garage

kitchen

dining

bedroom

living

entry

library

FIRST
FLOOR

·DOORS·

bedroom

bedroom

SECOND
FLOOR

·FRONT· (SOUTH·FOR·SOLAR)

RIGHT

PALA'OMAWKI: RED·HOUSE·
·PLATE·23·

PLATE 23

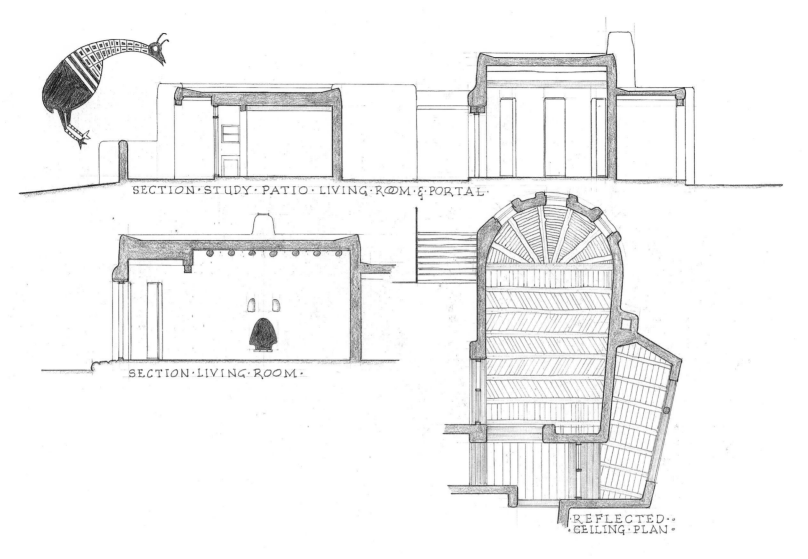

SECTION·STUDY·PATIO·LIVING·ROOM·&·PORTAL·

SECTION·LIVING·ROOM·

·REFLECTED·
·CEILING·PLAN·

·QÖCHATUWA·

PLATE 24. *White Sand*

White Sand is a single-story design that separates the living room from kitchen and dining areas and from the private bedroom areas of the home. This project integrates interior patios into the separation and delineation of functional areas within the dwelling. The adobe walls create nonrectilinear rooms and emphasize the sculptural qualities of this building material. The reflected ceiling plan reaffirms the abstraction of the design and open structure of the residence.

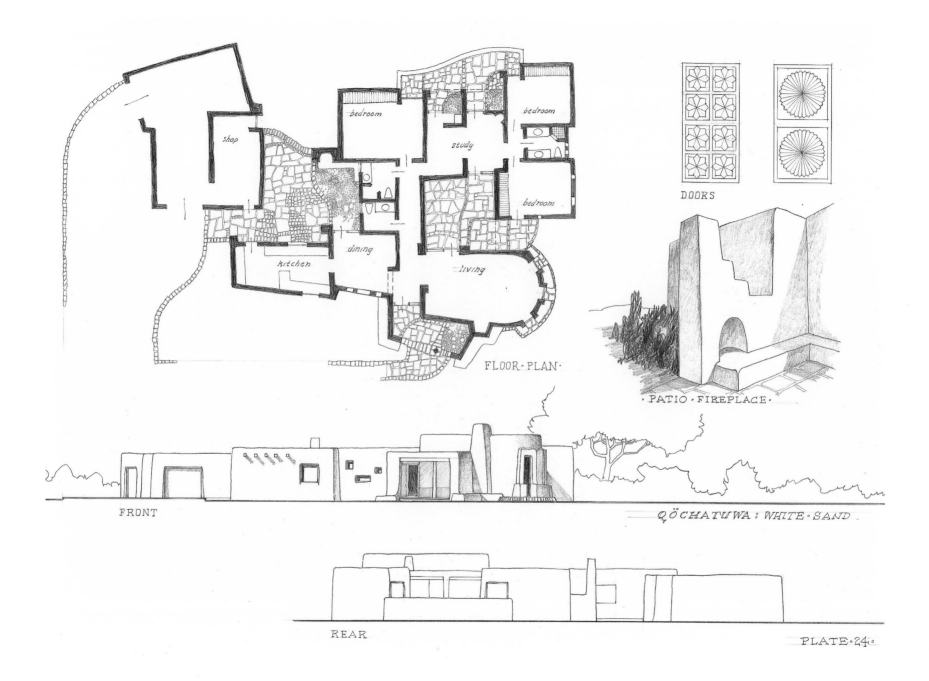

shop

bedroom

study

bedroom

bedroom

dining

kitchen

living

FLOOR·PLAN·

DOORS

·PATIO·FIREPLACE·

FRONT

QÖCHATUWA: WHITE·SAND

REAR

PLATE·24·

PLATE 24

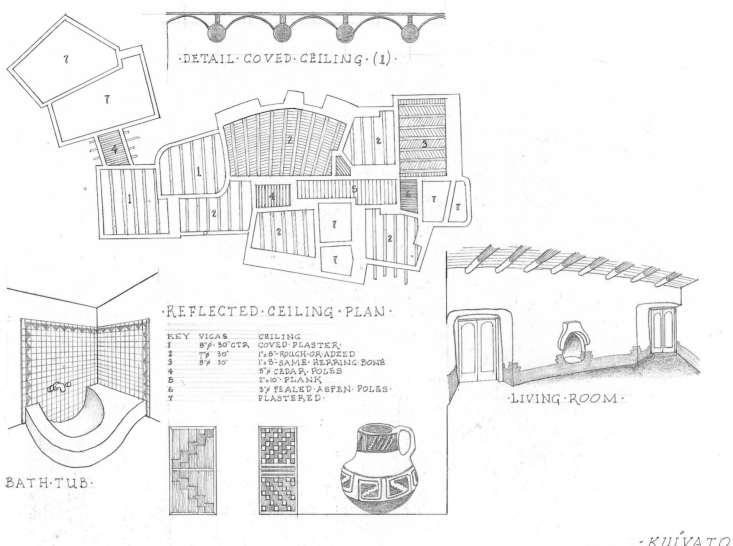

·DETAIL·COVED·CEILING·(1)·

·REFLECTED·CEILING·PLAN·

KEY	VIGAS	CEILING
1	8"∅·30"CTR.	COVED·PLASTER·
2	7"∅ 30"	1"x8"-ROUGH-OR-ADZED
3	8"∅ 30"	1"x8"-SAME-HERRING·BONE
4		5"∅ CEDAR·POLES
5		2"x10"·PLANK
6		3"∅ PEALED·ASPEN·POLES·
7		PLASTERED·

·BATH·TUB·

·LIVING·ROOM·

·KUÍVATO·

PLATE 25. *Greeting the Sun*

Greeting the Sun presents another single-story adobe residence organized as a nonrectilinear open study. Entrance through a portal leads directly into the core of the house—the living room—whose walls emphasize transitions to patios, to the exterior, or to the dining room. The adobe is used as a highly plastic, sculptural building material. The flagstone patios and stonemasonry walls help to minimize the distinction between interior and exterior spaces.

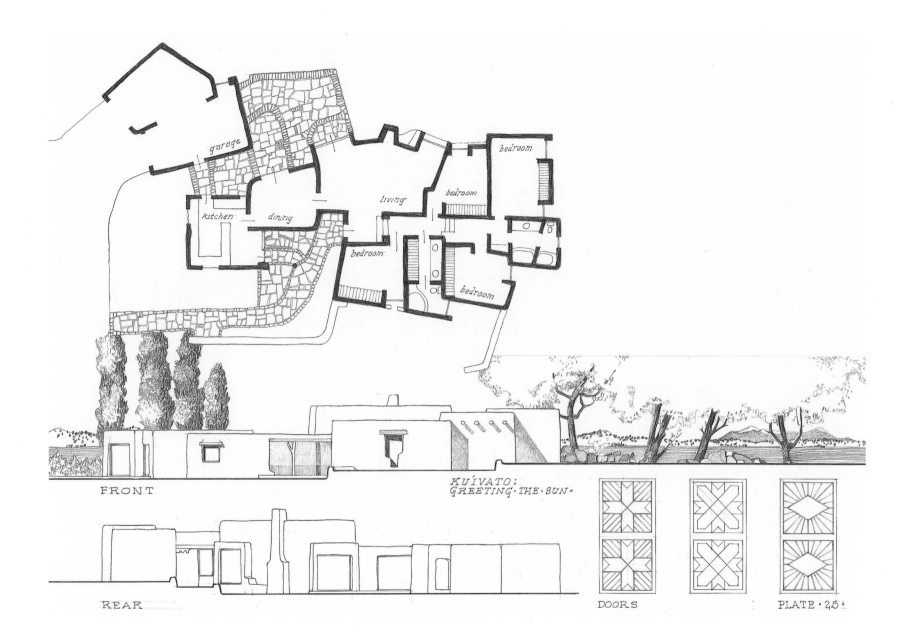

garage

kitchen   dining

living

bedroom

bedroom

bedroom

bedroom

bedroom

FRONT

KUÍVATO:
GREETING·THE·SUN·

REAR

DOORS

PLATE·25·

PLATE 25

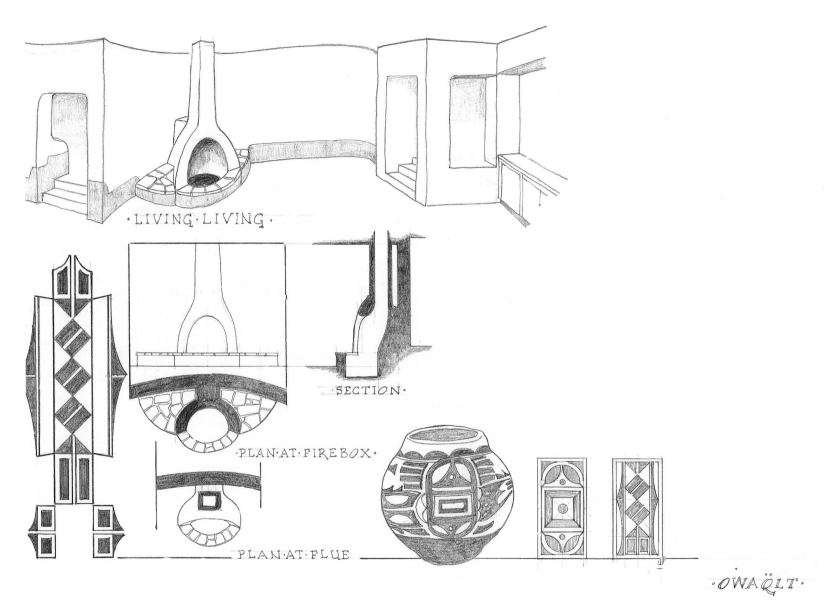

· LIVING · LIVING ·

· SECTION ·

· PLAN · AT · FIREBOX ·

· PLAN · AT · FLUE ·

· OWAQLT ·

PLATE 26. *Scattered Rocks*

Scattered Rocks presents a single-story adobe residence based on an arching layout and the absence of rectilinear rooms.[27] The sculptural walls are built from a combination of stone, adobe, and glass to minimize the distinction between the house itself and the surrounding environment. Details, including a massive fireplace in the living room and doors incorporating Pueblo designs into their structure, ground this flowing design in visual icons of the Southwest.

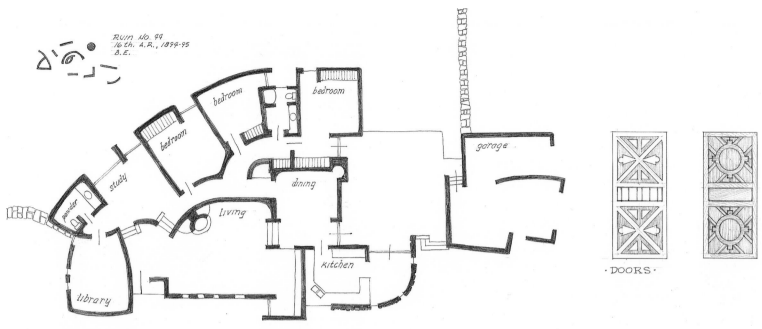

Ruin No. 44
16th. A.R., 1894-95
B.E.

bedroom

bedroom

bedroom

study

garage

powder

dining

living

kitchen

library

· FLOOR · PLAN ·

· DOORS ·

· FRONT ·

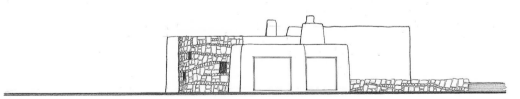

· RIGHT · SIDE ·

O WAQLT : SCATTERED · ROCKS ·
· PLATE · 26 ·

PLATE 26

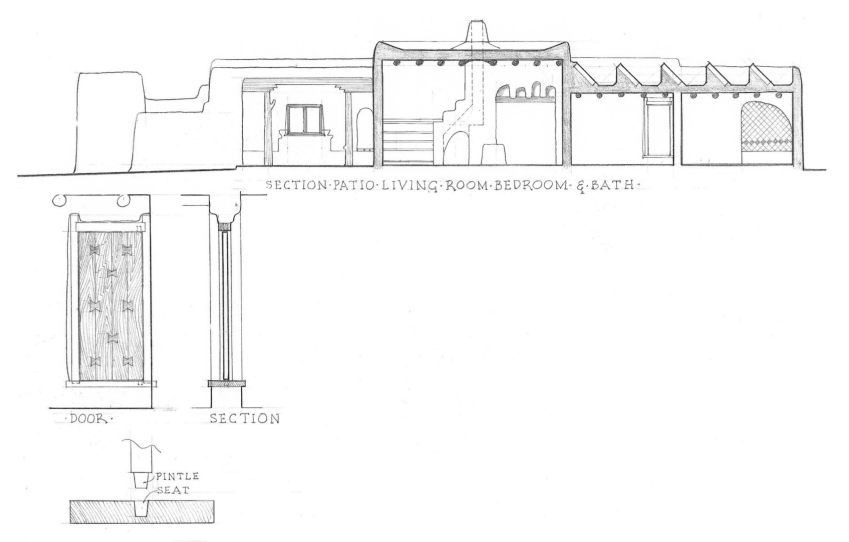

·SECTION·PATIO·LIVING·ROOM·BEDROOM·&·BATH·

·DOOR·   SECTION

PINTLE
SEAT

·MUMURVA·

PLATE 27. *Water Grass Place*

Water Grass Place is another single-story asymmetrical residence that Lumpkins based on the floor plan of White House, a prehistoric pueblo ruin at Canyon de Chelly.[28] The source design emphasizes the development of the pueblo through accretion. Lumpkins creates a modern project that maintains the look of building through accumulation. This project also incorporates the handmade details that define this series of designs, including integrated patios, asymmetrical windows, hand-joined doors, and a prodigious fireplace in the living room.

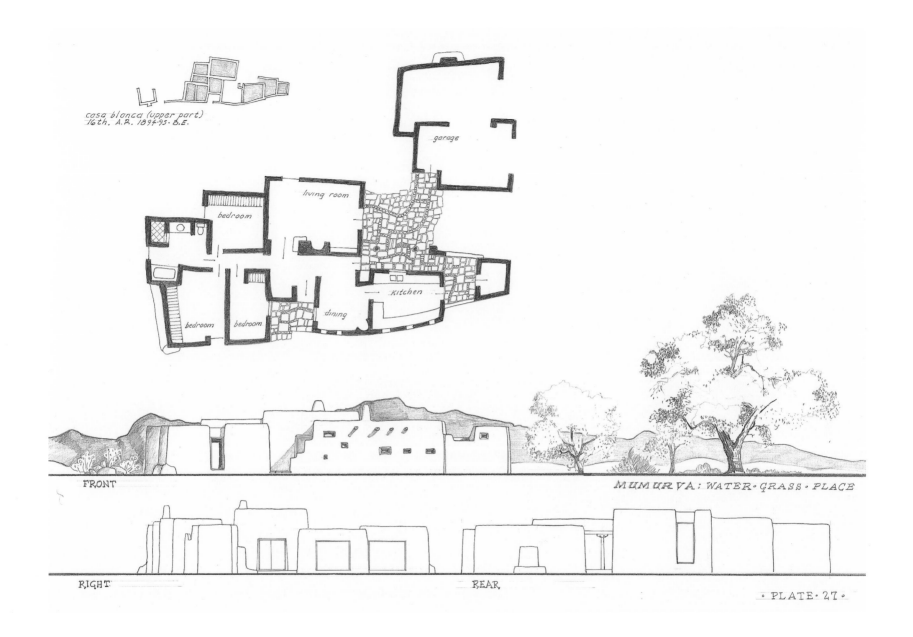

casa blanca (upper part)
16th. A.B. 1894-95. B.E.

garage

living room

bedroom

bedroom   bedroom   dining   kitchen

FRONT

MUMURVA: WATER · GRASS · PLACE

RIGHT

REAR

· PLATE · 27 ·

PLATE 27

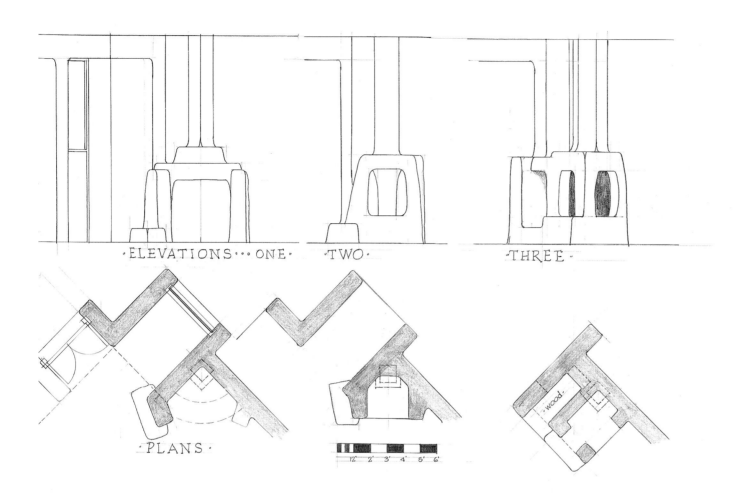

·ELEVATIONS···ONE· ·TWO· ·THREE·

·PLANS·

·wood·

1' 2' 3' 4' 5' 6'

PLATE 28. *Circle*

This symmetrical interpretation of a prehistoric ruin in Canyon de Chelly, in eastern Arizona, is based on a great kiva embedded within a block of rectilinear rooms.[29] Three wings of rooms radiate from a circular courtyard that anchors this design. The living room is placed directly across from the entrance at the rear of the courtyard, a structural arrangement that blends the central courtyard from Lumpkins's Spanish-Pueblo designs. A wing of bedrooms and private rooms extends to the left from the courtyard while the kitchen and dining areas are placed in the wing to the right of the entrance. A circular hallway surrounding the courtyard connects private spaces with the living room and the dining and kitchen area.

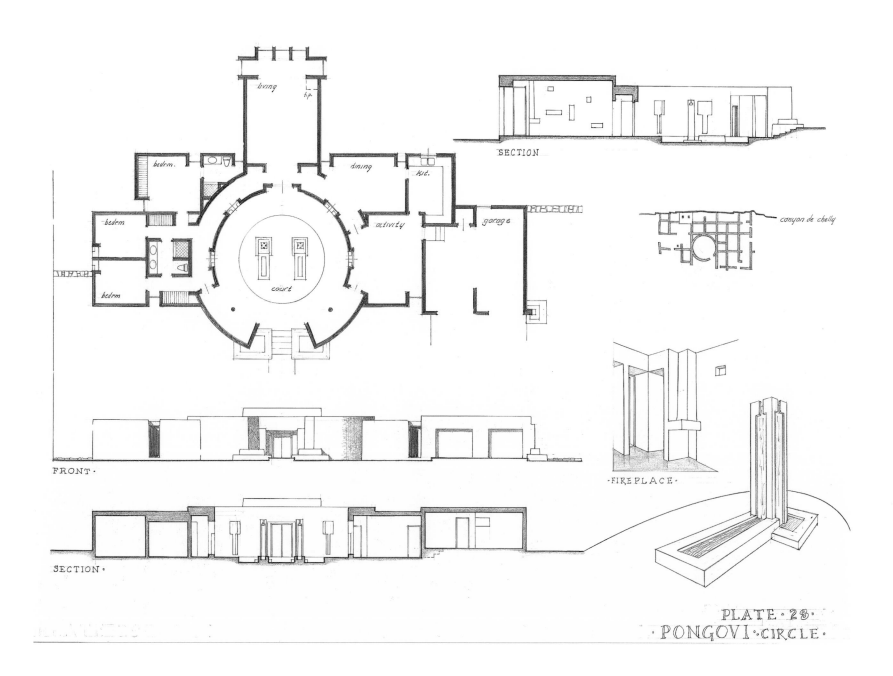

living

t.p.

bedrm.

dining

kit.

bedrm

activity

garage

court

bedrm

SECTION

canyon de chelly

FRONT·

SECTION·

·FIREPLACE·

PLATE ·28·
·PONGOVI ·CIRCLE·

PLATE 28

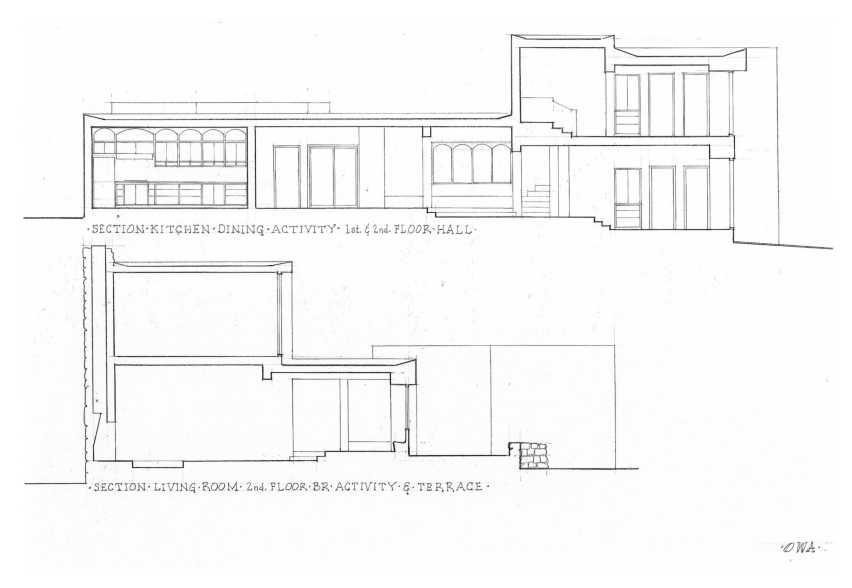

·SECTION·KITCHEN·DINING·ACTIVITY· 1st. & 2nd. FLOOR·HALL·

·SECTION· LIVING·ROOM· 2nd. FLOOR·BR·ACTIVITY· & TERRACE·

·OWA·

PLATE 29. *Rock*

Rock presents a one- and two-story residence that combines both adobe and stone-masonry construction. Formally Lumpkins again relies on the ground plan of the upper part of White House Ruin for the internal relationships within the residence.[30] This layout does not split public and private aspects of dwelling as clearly as in most of his projects but instead seems to concentrate on the exterior relationships between adobe and stone construction materials. The entrance leads into the center of an asymmetrically organized unit that combines the kitchen, breakfast nook, dining room, activity room, and living room. While Lumpkins includes two bedrooms on the first floor, the core of the private areas is placed on the second floor. The curved stone tower dominates the exterior of the residence and includes the chimney for the fireplace in the living room on the first floor and the fireplace for the master bedroom on the second floor.

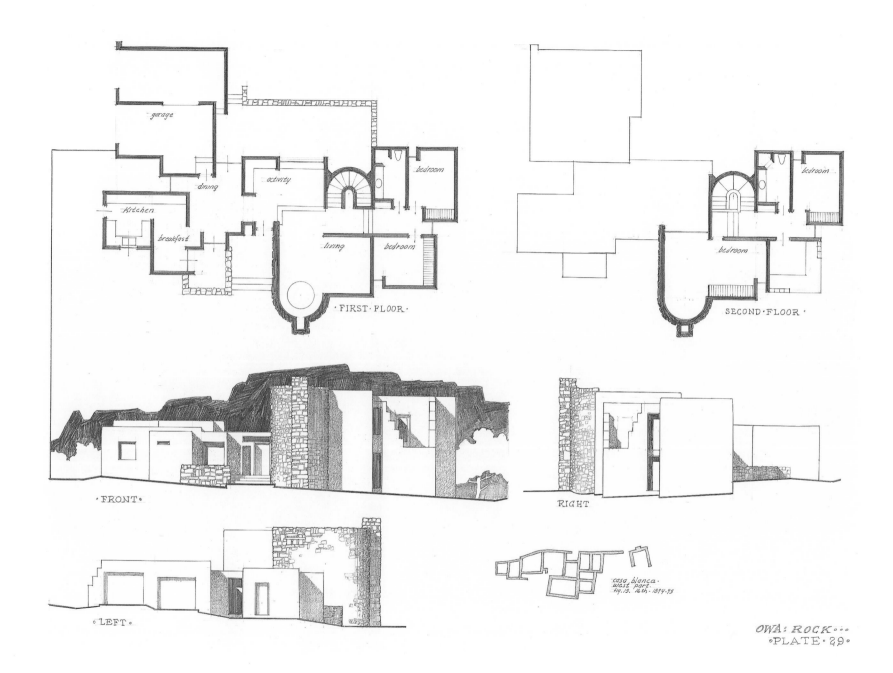

garage

dining   activity   bedroom

Kitchen

breakfast   living   bedroom

FIRST·FLOOR·

bedroom

bedroom

SECOND·FLOOR·

·FRONT·

RIGHT

·LEFT·

casa blanca
west part.
fig. 13. 16th. 1894-95

OWA: ROCK···
·PLATE·29·

PLATE 29

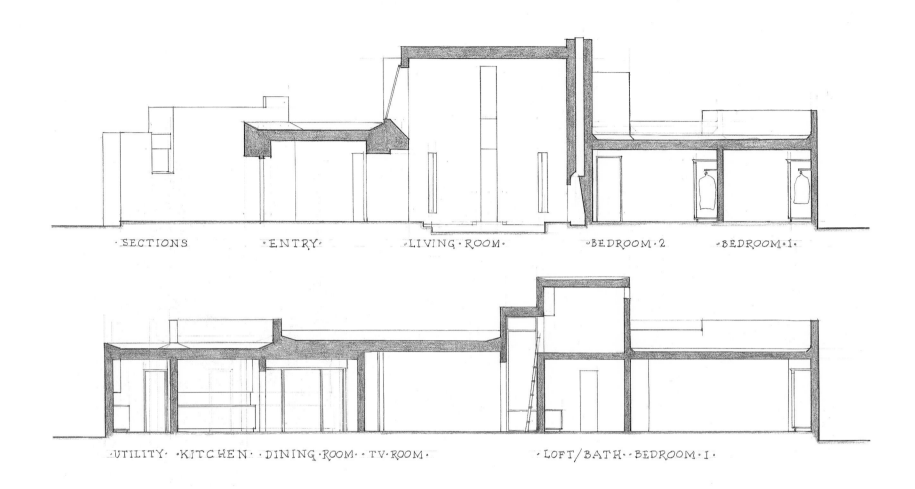

·SECTIONS·   ·ENTRY·   ·LIVING·ROOM·   ·BEDROOM·2·   ·BEDROOM·1·

·UTILITY·KITCHEN·DINING·ROOM·TV·ROOM·   ·LOFT/BATH·BEDROOM·1·

PLATE 30. *Kachina House*

Lumpkins based this *Kachina House* design on a floor plan from a prehistoric Pueblo dwelling found in Canyon de Chelly.[31] The asymmetry of the source structure comes from fitting the construction into a cliff face. Lumpkins constructs an entrance for *Kachina House* at the juncture between two rectilinear floor plan grids taken from the source layout. The circular kiva in the prehistoric dwelling becomes a two-story living room in Lumpkins's design and serves as the focus of his modern layout. The bench from the kiva in the source layout is repeated by Lumpkins as a *banco* in the living room of *Kachina House*.

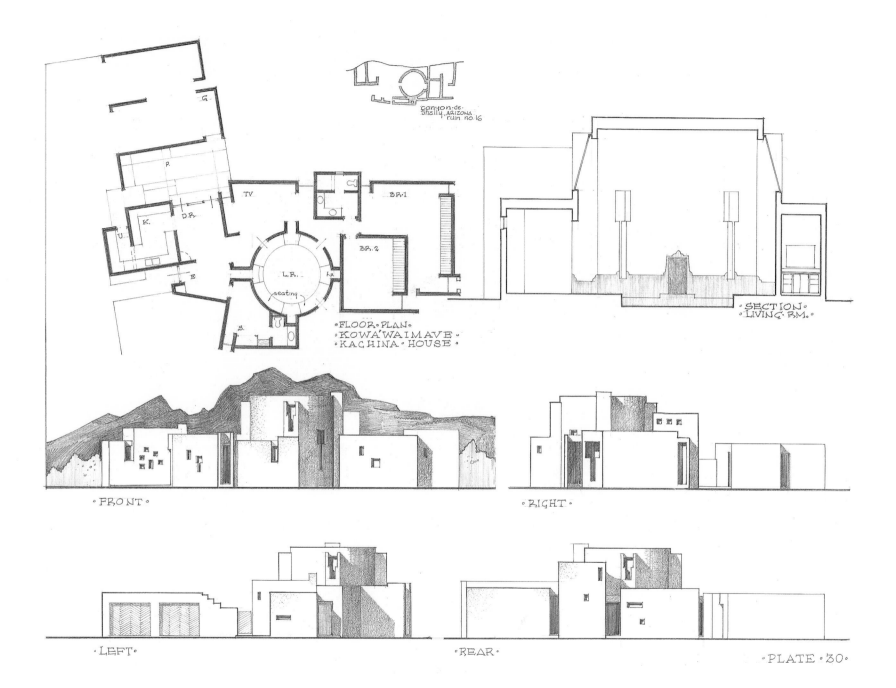

canyon·de·
Shelly·ARIZONA·
ruin no.16

·FLOOR·PLAN·
·KOWA'WAIMAVE·
·KACHINA·HOUSE·

G.
P.
TV.
K.
D.B.
U.
E.
S.
L.R.
seating
f.p.
BR.1
BR.2

·SECTION·
·LIVING·RM.·

·FRONT·

·RIGHT·

·LEFT·

·REAR·

·PLATE·30·

PLATE 30

·SECTION·LIVING·ROOM·

·SECTION·BATH·ROOMS·&·COURT·

·GARDEN·ELEVATION·

PLATE 31. *House of the Animal Kingdom*

House of the Animal Kingdom continues to use kivas as a source for the core of Lumpkins's symmetrical, modern designs.[32] The public and private areas radiate from a circular courtyard at the heart of the design. Unlike other designs based on prehistoric layouts, this single-story project is highly structured and formally arranged around the courtyard. The large living room and fireplace are located across from the entrance through the courtyard.

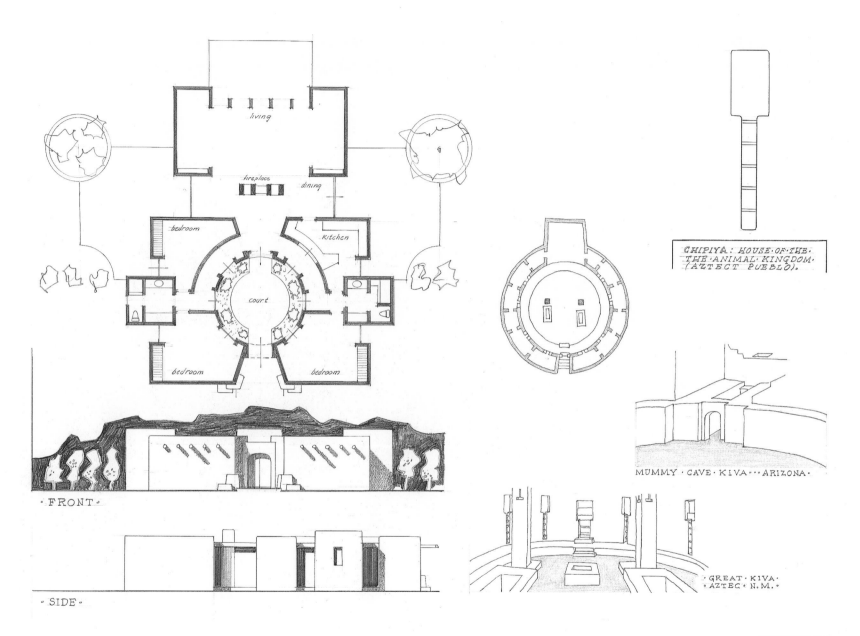

living

fireplace   dining

bedroom   kitchen

court

bedroom   bedroom

· FRONT ·

· SIDE ·

CHIPIYA : HOUSE · OF · THE ·
THE · ANIMAL · KINGDOM ·
(AZTECT PUEBLO).

MUMMY · CAVE · KIVA · · · ARIZONA ·

· GREAT · KIVA ·
· AZTEC · N.M. ·

PLATE · 31 ·

PLATE 31

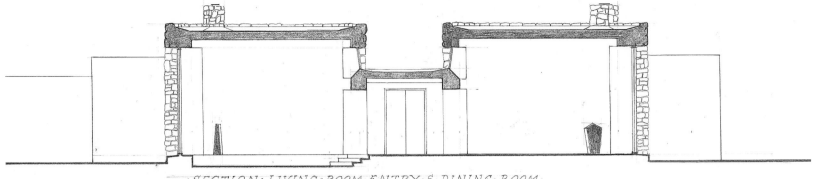

·SECTION·LIVING·ROOM·ENTRY·&·DINING·ROOM·

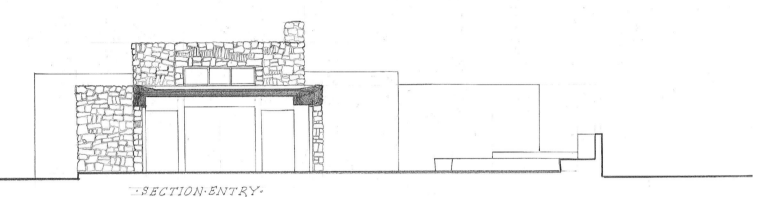

·SECTION·ENTRY·

·TALA'NUMTIWA·

PLATE 32. *Sun Covering the Land*

Sun Covering the Land expands the formal grid of rectilinear rooms surrounding a circular courtyard that Lumpkins investigated in the previous project (plate 31). Structurally, *Sun Covering the Land* appears as two units arranged along a central entranceway. The new layout emphasizes an equivalence between a circular living room on one side of the building and a similar circular dining area on the other side. The use of stonemasonry emphasizes the central role of the living room and dining area in this design.

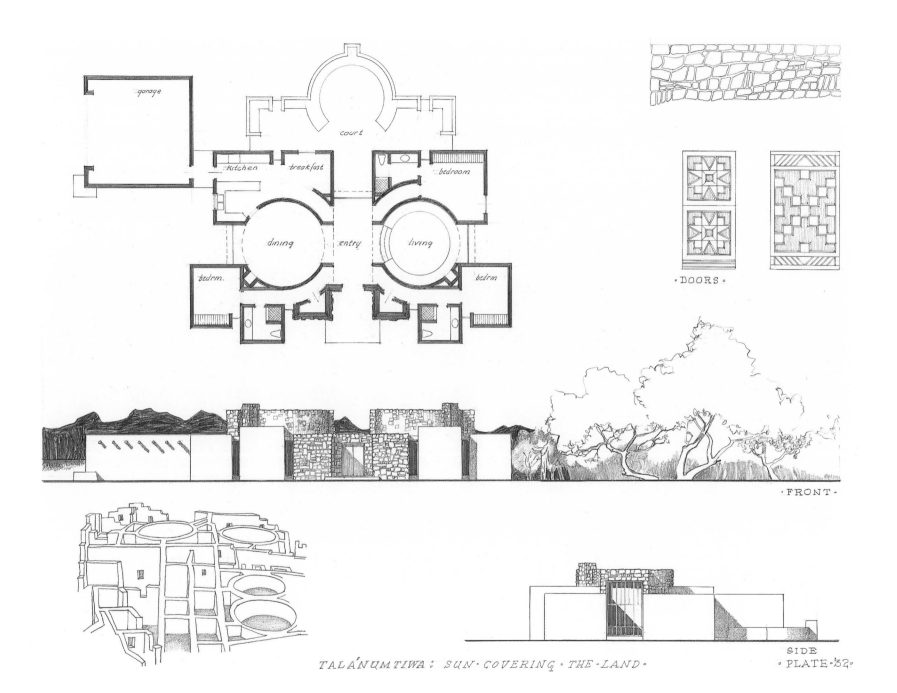

garage

court

kitchen · breakfast · bedroom

dining · entry · living

bedrm. · bedrm

· DOORS ·

· FRONT ·

TALA´NUMTIWA : SUN · COVERING · THE · LAND ·

SIDE

· PLATE · 32 ·

PLATE 32

PLATE 33. *Cloud House*

Cloud House is a pared-down version of Lumpkins's previous project *Sun Covering the Land* (plate 32). By removing some of the rooms and adding a bedroom wing off the living room, *Cloud House* becomes an asymmetric design that seems more in concert with the rest of Lumpkins's series of designs. The stonemasonry focuses attention on the entrance and forms a strong contrast with the adobe used in the remainder of the building.

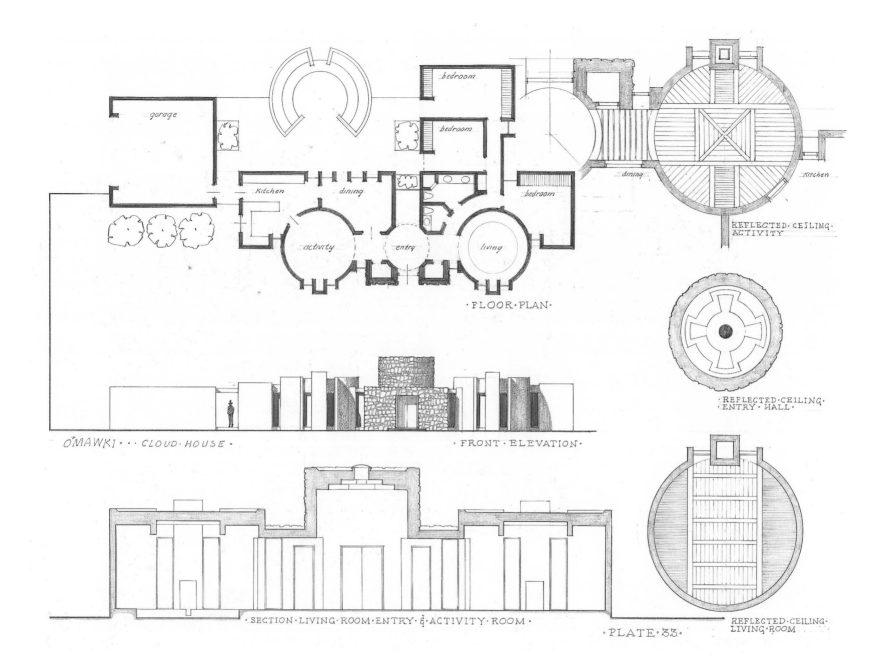

garage

bedroom

bedroom

bedroom

kitchen dining

activity entry living

·FLOOR·PLAN·

dining kitchen

·REFLECTED·CEILING·
ACTIVITY·

·REFLECTED·CEILING·
·ENTRY·HALL·

O'MAWKI···CLOUD·HOUSE· ·FRONT·ELEVATION·

·SECTION·LIVING·ROOM·ENTRY·&·ACTIVITY·ROOM· ·PLATE·33· REFLECTED·CEILING·
LIVING·ROOM·

PLATE 33

PLATE 34.
Earth Painted with Green Plants

Earth Painted with Green Plants expands previous designs that include circular courtyards or circular rooms incorporated into rectilinear room blocks.[33] Although this plan shares its source materials with those found in plate 28, this project creates an asymmetrical design that segregates public areas to the left of the entrance and private areas to the back and the right of the entrance. These distinctions are further emphasized by changes in floor height and steps leading to each area. This design returns to a sculptural use of adobe, flagstone patios, and the use of stonemasonry for the circular entrance room in the center of the building. Shadows cast from the portal against the adobe walls emphasize the entrance to the building.

·ALTERNATE·F.P.·

·SECTION·DINING·LIVING·ROOM·ENTRY·&·BEDROOM·

·ALT·F.P.·

·KUWA'NVENOMA·

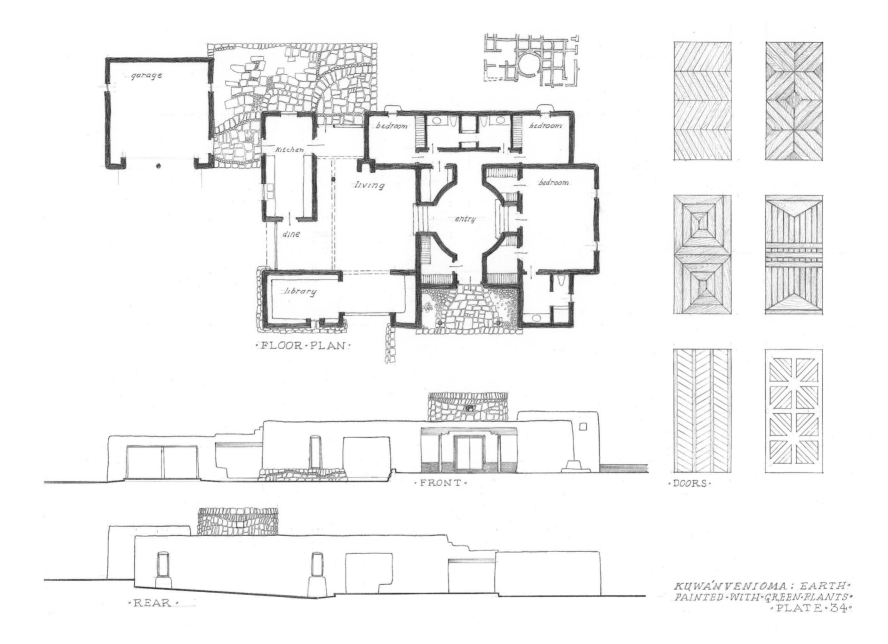

·FLOOR·PLAN·

garage

kitchen

bedroom

bedroom

living

bedroom

dine

entry

library

·FRONT·

·REAR·

·DOORS·

*KUWA'NVENIOMA: EARTH·
PAINTED·WITH·GREEN·PLANTS·
·PLATE·34·*

PLATE 34

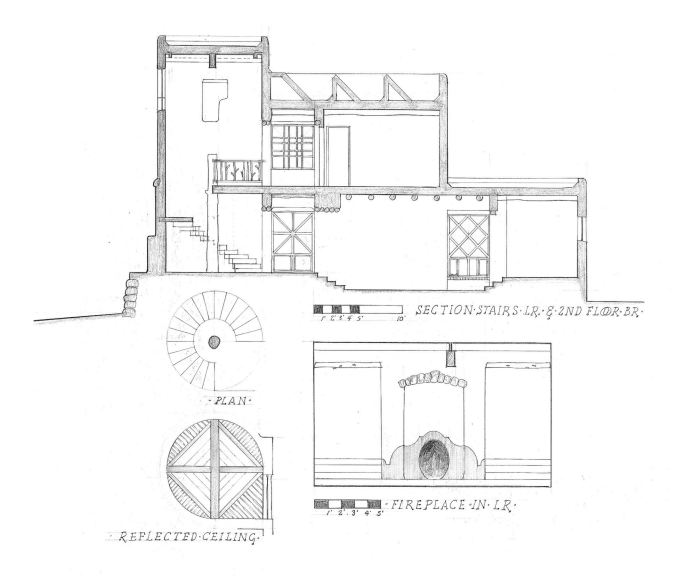

·SECTION·STAIRS·LR·&·2ND·FLOOR·BR·

1 2' 3' 4' 5'   10'

·PLAN·

·REFLECTED·CEILING·

·FIREPLACE·IN·LR·

1 2' 3' 4' 5'

PLATE 35. *Deer*

In *Deer*, Lumpkins reinvestigates the asymmetric layouts seen in the previous design by combining round masonry towers, two-story adobe room blocks, flagstone patios defined by low partition walls, and details marked by Puebloesque designs, T-windows, and asymmetrical fenestration. The exterior look of the project resembles the look of the Cliff Palace ruin at Mesa Verde National Park in Colorado, which Lumpkins replicates as an elevation study on the plan.

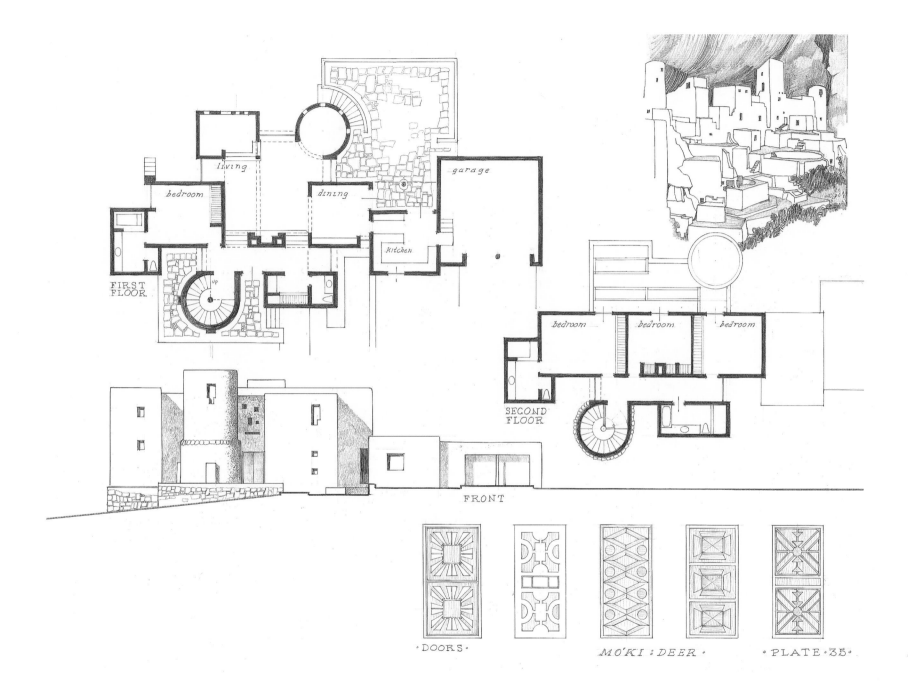

FIRST
FLOOR

living

bedroom

dining

garage

kitchen

up

SECOND
FLOOR

bedroom   bedroom   bedroom

FRONT

·DOORS·   *MO'KI : DEER*   ·PLATE·35·

PLATE 35

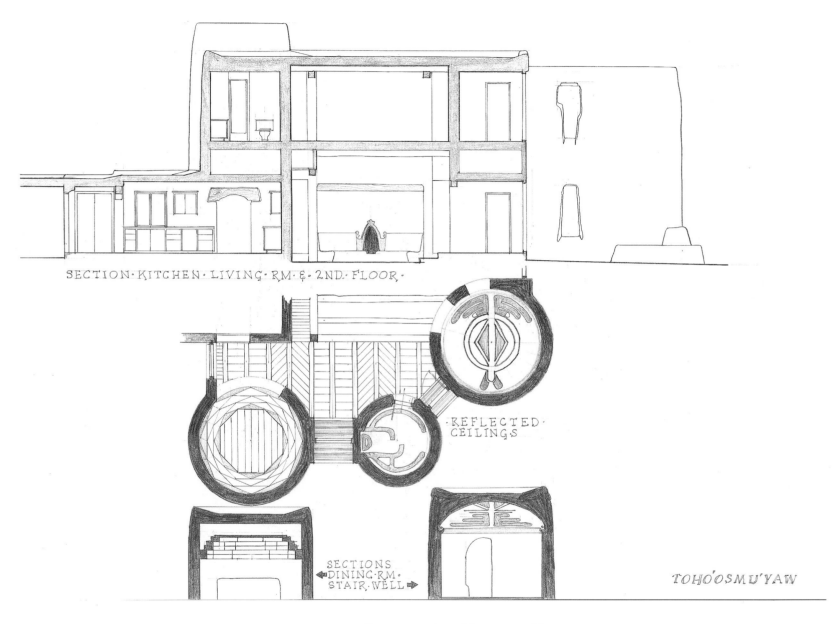

SECTION·KITCHEN·LIVING·RM·&·2ND·FLOOR·

·REFLECTED·
CEILINGS

SECTIONS
DINING·RM·
STAIR·WELL

TOHO'OSMU'YAW

PLATE 36. *Harvest Moon*

Lumpkins abandons rectilinear room blocks in favor of circular stonemasonry towers in this two-story project. The design features five such towers. The kitchen, breakfast nook, dining area, and living room open directly from the entrance. The bedroom blocks branch from a circular tower containing the circular staircase connecting the two levels of private spaces. The circular towers are roofed by overlapping beams as in prehistoric kivas or modern Navajo hogans.

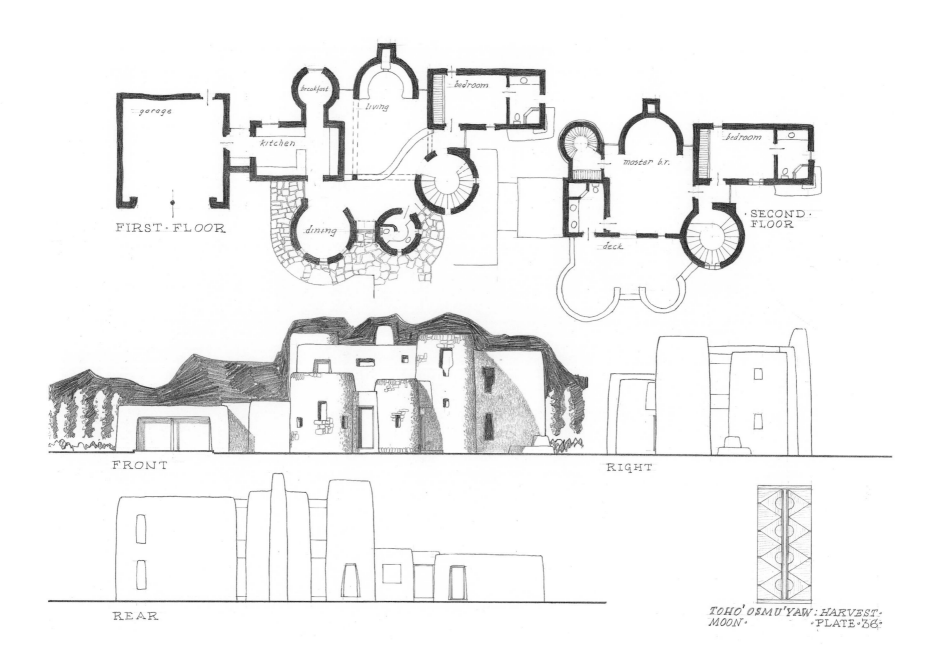

FIRST·FLOOR

garage

kitchen

breakfast

living

dining

bedroom

SECOND
FLOOR

master b.r.

bedroom

deck

FRONT

RIGHT

REAR

TOHO'OSMU'YAW: HARVEST·
MOON· ·PLATE·36·

PLATE 36

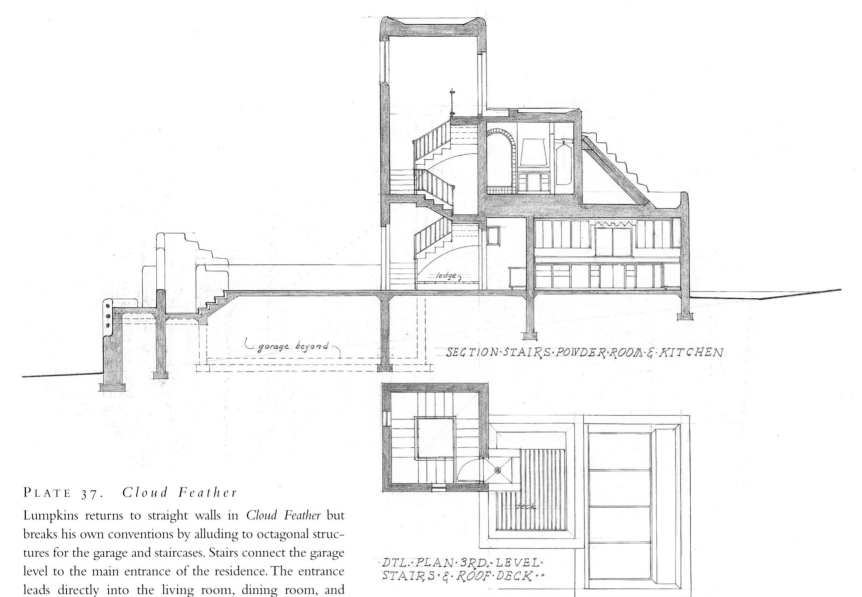

SECTION·STAIRS·POWDER·ROOM·&·KITCHEN

garage beyond

ledge

DTL.·PLAN·3RD.·LEVEL·
STAIRS·&·ROOF·DECK··

deck

···OMAWNAKW···

PLATE 37. *Cloud Feather*

Lumpkins returns to straight walls in *Cloud Feather* but breaks his own conventions by alluding to octagonal structures for the garage and staircases. Stairs connect the garage level to the main entrance of the residence. The entrance leads directly into the living room, dining room, and kitchen, which are all on one level. The bedrooms are on different levels, which psychologically helps to separate private and public areas. The differing levels of the residence accentuate the height of the second-floor bedrooms and the high height of the living room on the first floor. Despite the height of this project, it does not look as massive as other homes in this series.

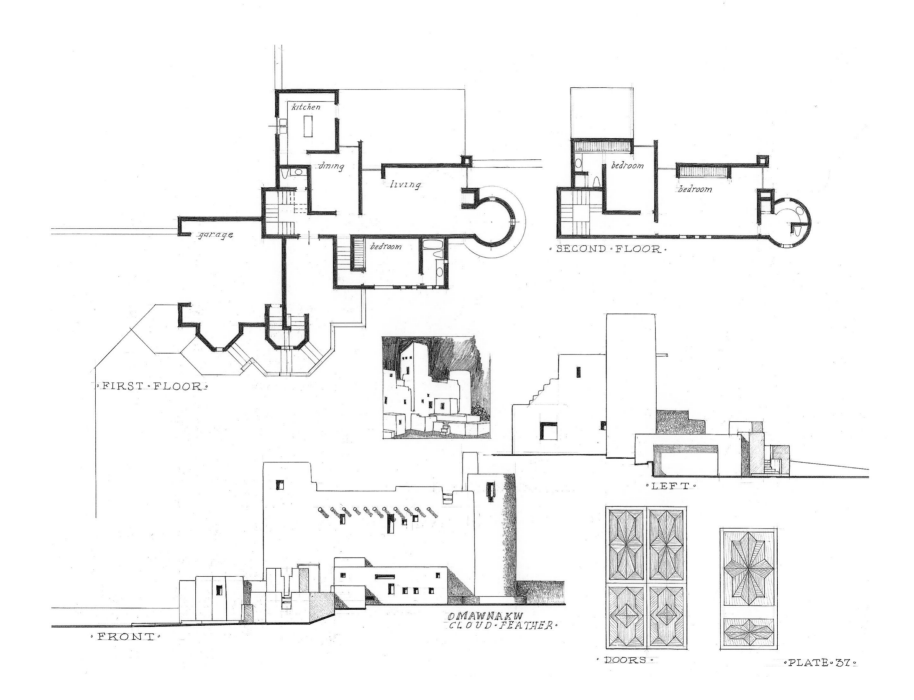

kitchen

dining

living

garage

bedroom

·SECOND·FLOOR·

bedroom

bedroom

·FIRST·FLOOR·

·LEFT·

·FRONT·

OMAWNAKW
CLOUD·FEATHER·

·DOORS·

·PLATE·37·

PLATE 37

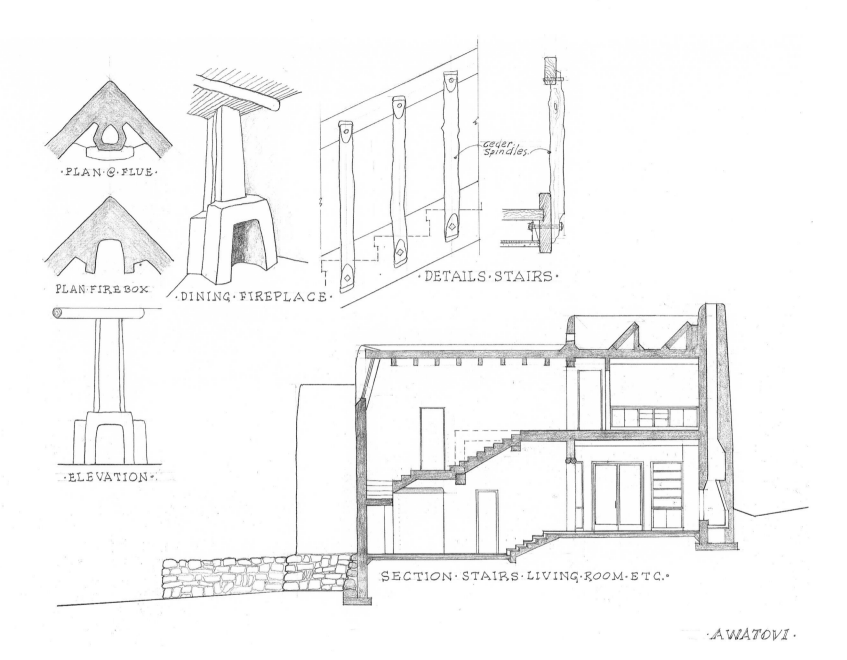

·PLAN·@·FLUE·

·PLAN·FIRE BOX·

·DINING·FIREPLACE·

ceder spindles.

·DETAILS·STAIRS·

·ELEVATION·

·SECTION·STAIRS·LIVING·ROOM·ETC.·

·AWATOVI·

PLATE 38.
Place of the Bow—Montezuma's Castle

Lumpkins developed the facades for *Place of the Bow* from the prehistoric ruin Montezuma's Castle in northern Arizona. The basic layout for this project refines many of the ideas explored in previous designs in this series but seems more conventional than most. The massive two-story residence segregates the kitchen, dining room, and living room on the first floor from the bedrooms and private spaces on the second floor.

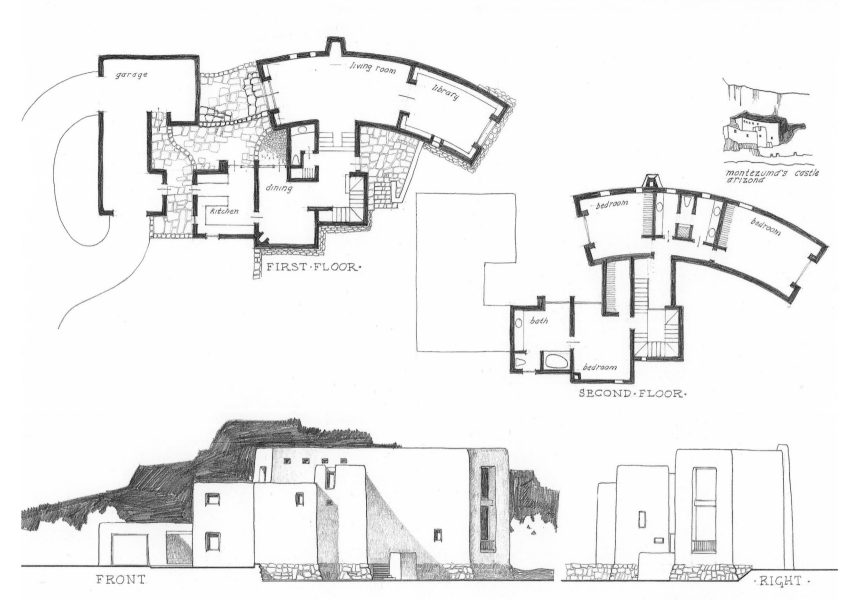

garage

living room

library

dining

kitchen

FIRST·FLOOR·

montezuma's castle
arizona

bedroom

bedroom

bath

bedroom

SECOND·FLOOR·

FRONT

RIGHT·

AWATOVI: PLACE·OF·THE·BOW
·PLATE·38·

PLATE 38

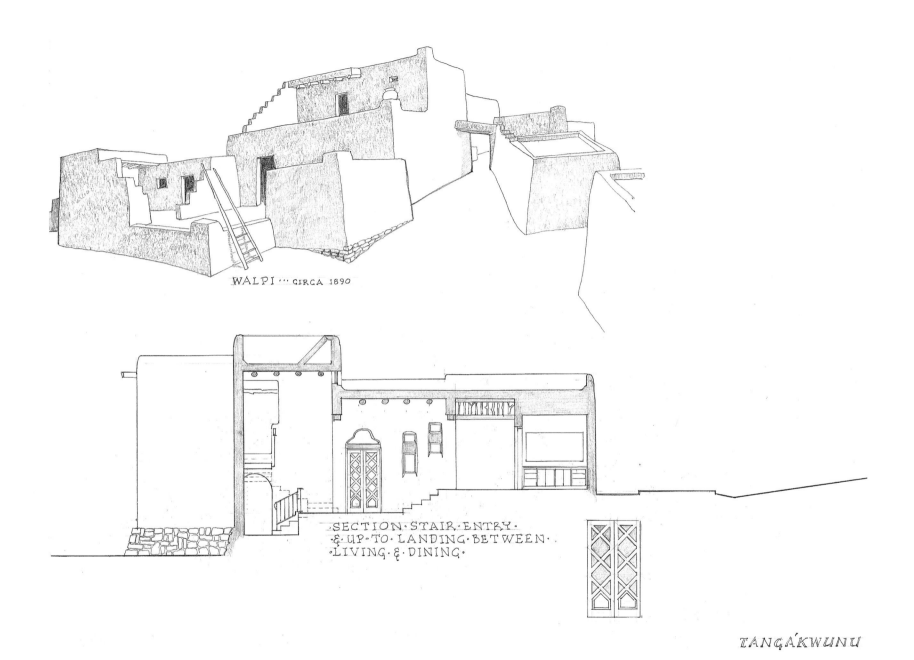

WALPI ·· CIRCA 1890

·SECTION·STAIR·ENTRY·
·& UP·TO·LANDING·BETWEEN·
·LIVING·&·DINING·

TANGÁKWUNU

PLATE 39. *Rainbow*

Lumpkins experiments with the separation of public and private areas in his project *Rainbow*. He accentuates this distinction by modeling the private spaces as conventional rectilinear rooms and by creating public spaces as curved rooms. The arced public rooms radiate from the entranceway and the open patios that separate the public and private areas. The private bedrooms on the first floor are reached by walking down several steps, while the second-story bedrooms and the deck retreat are reached by walking up a flight of stairs.

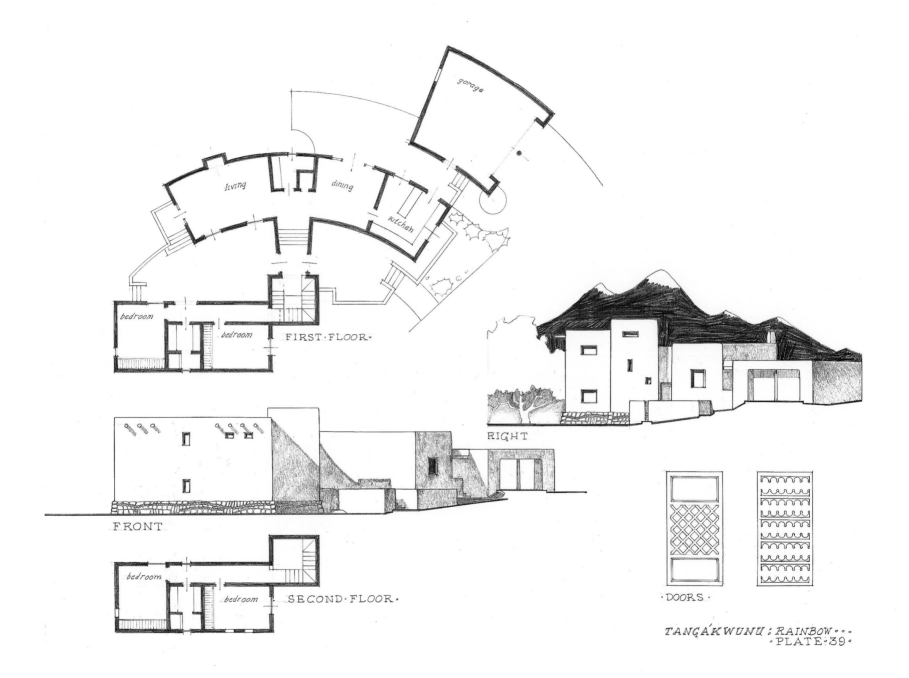

living

dining

kitchen

garage

bedroom

bedroom

FIRST·FLOOR·

RIGHT

FRONT

bedroom

bedroom

SECOND·FLOOR·

·DOORS·

TANGÁKWUNU : RAINBOW · · ·
·PLATE·39·

PLATE 39

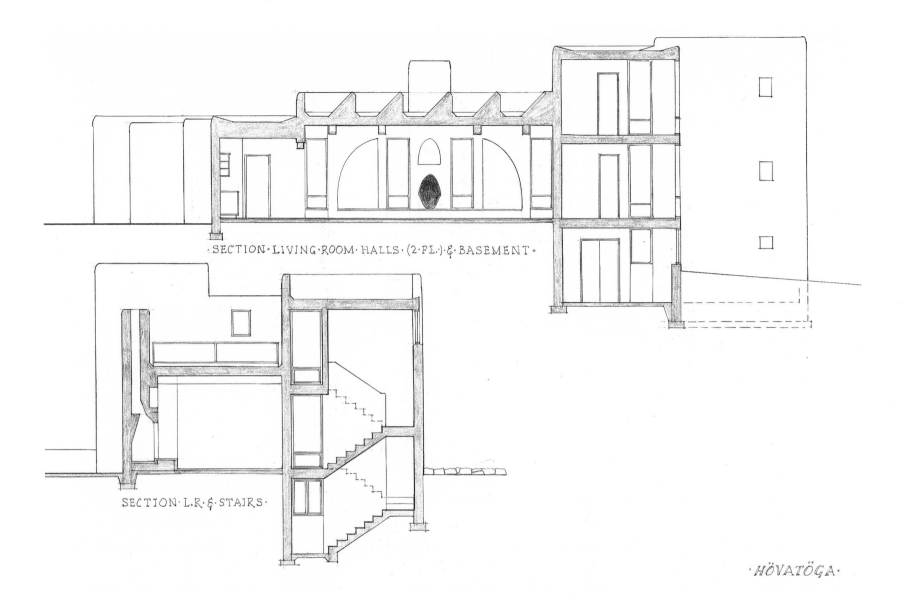

·SECTION·LIVING·ROOM·HALLS·(2·FL·)·&·BASEMENT·

·SECTION·L.R·&·STAIRS·

·HÖVATÖGA·

PLATE 40. *Cut in the Cliff*

Lumpkins returns to an interest in the exterior of his projects in *Cut in the Cliff*. He incorporates windows placed between sections of adobe to emphasize the separation between two-story room blocks. The asymmetry of T-windows and the placement of smaller windows prevent the facades from becoming blank faces of stucco. The cuts in the adobe facades emphasize the vertical elements in the design and prevent this large structure from seeming ponderous.

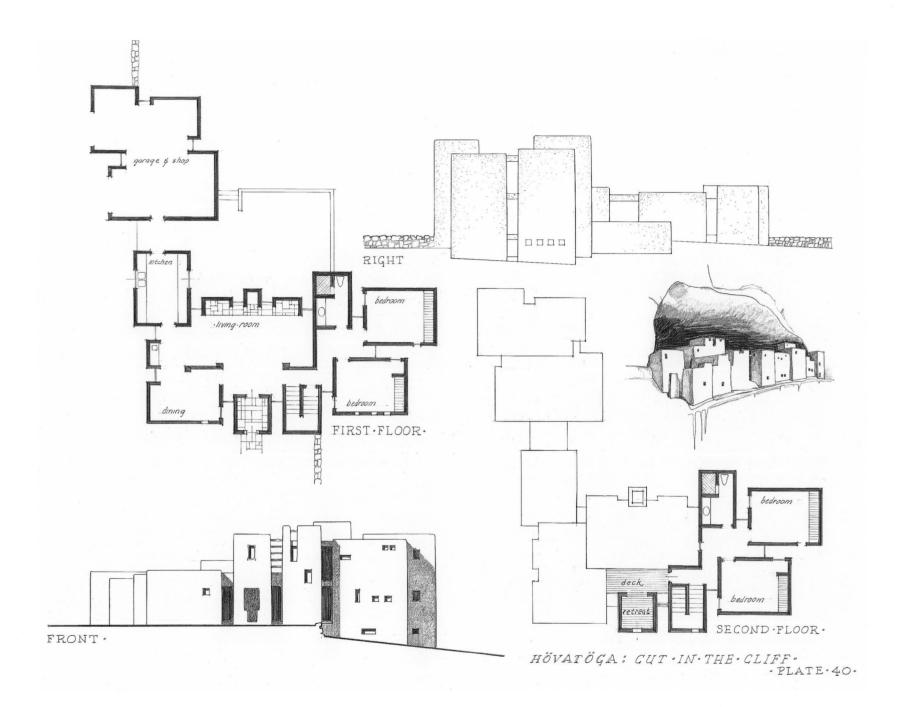

garage & shop

kitchen

·living·room·

bedroom

dining

bedroom

FIRST·FLOOR·

RIGHT

bedroom

deck

retreat

bedroom

SECOND·FLOOR·

FRONT·

HÖVATÖGA: CUT·IN·THE·CLIFF
·PLATE·40·

PLATE 40

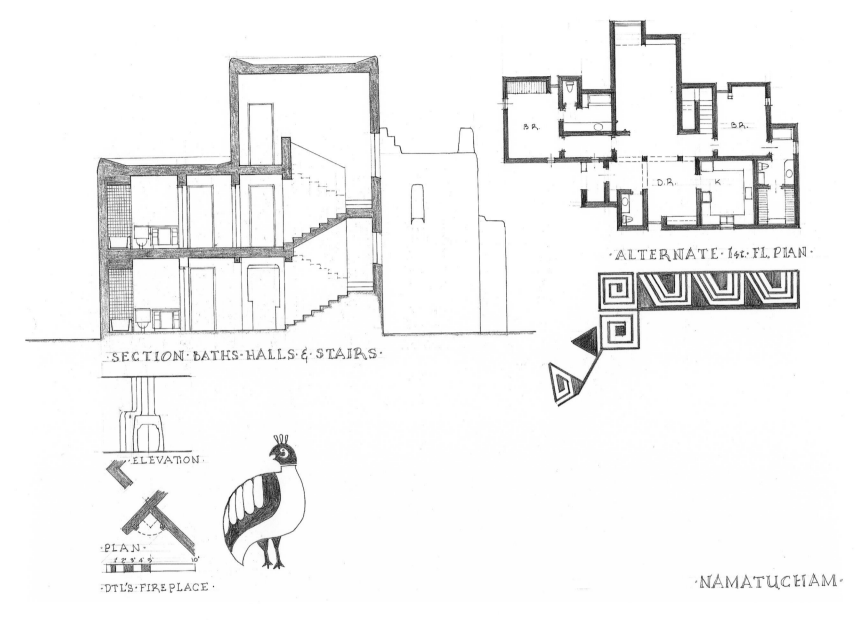

·SECTION·BATHS·HALLS·&·STAIRS·

·ELEVATION·

·PLAN·

·DTL'S·FIREPLACE·

·ALTERNATE·1st·FL·PLAN·

BR.

BR.

DR.

K

·NAMATUCHAM·

PLATE 41. *Invitation to the Home*

Lumpkins explores the blocky, two-story buildings found at Hopi and Zuni pueblos in his project *Invitation to the Home*. This layout looks like a conventional residence adapted to an adobe facade. The details, such as recessed vertical windows and segments between blocks of rooms, are not part of the facade of this project. Internally this design seems cramped and crowded because of the absence of internal courtyards and patios, which play such an important spatial and structural role in most of the designs in this series. Perhaps the most interesting part of this project is the second sheet, which details a selection of complex door patterns.

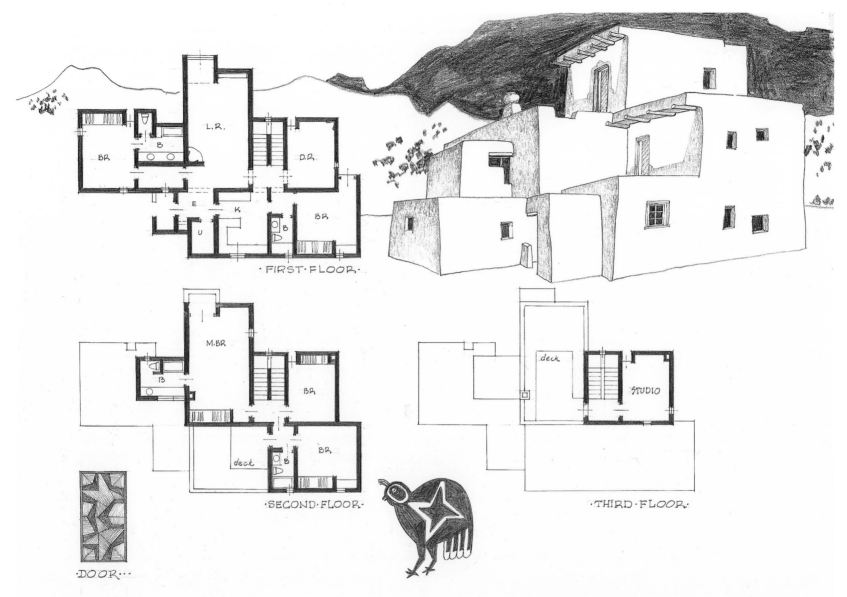

·FIRST·FLOOR·

L.R.

B

BR.

D.R.

E   K

U   B   BR.

·SECOND·FLOOR·

M.BR

B

BR.

deck   B   BR.

·THIRD·FLOOR·

deck   STUDIO

·DOOR·

·NAMATUCHAM· INVITATION TO THE HOME ·
·PLATE·41·

PLATE 41

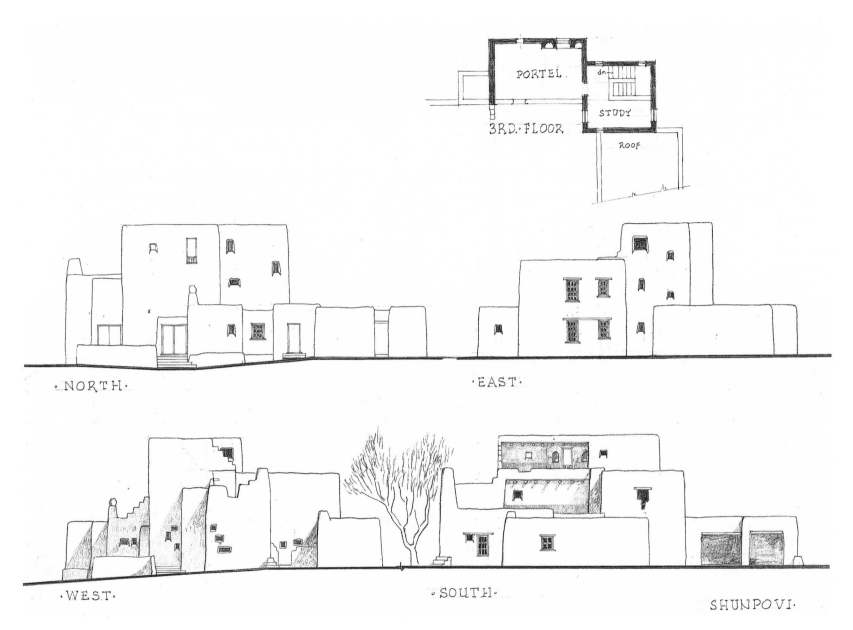

PORTEL

STUDY

dn

ROOF

3RD·FLOOR

·NORTH·

·EAST·

·WEST·

·SOUTH·

SHUNPOVI·

PLATE 42. *Shungopavi*

In *Shungopavi* Lumpkins opens the block-residence concept explored in plate 41 by adding interior and exterior courtyards. These additions, combined with details such as the shifted garage floor plan, make the facade more interesting. Simultaneously these changes create nooks within the home that reflect some of the aesthetic of Pueblo architecture from the last century.

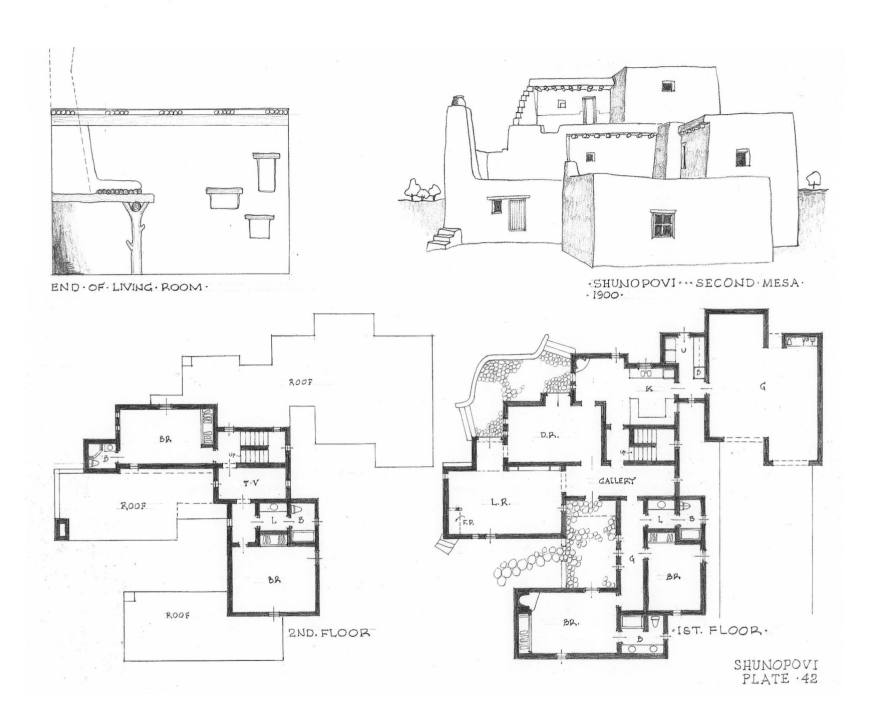

END · OF · LIVING · ROOM ·

· SHUNOPOVI · · · SECOND · MESA ·
· 1900 ·

ROOF

BR
B
UP
ROOF
T·V
L B
BR
ROOF
·2ND·FLOOR·

K
U
B
G
D·R·
UP
GALLERY
F.P.
L·R·
L B
G
BR
BR
B
·IST·FLOOR·

SHUNOPOVI
PLATE ·42

PLATE 42

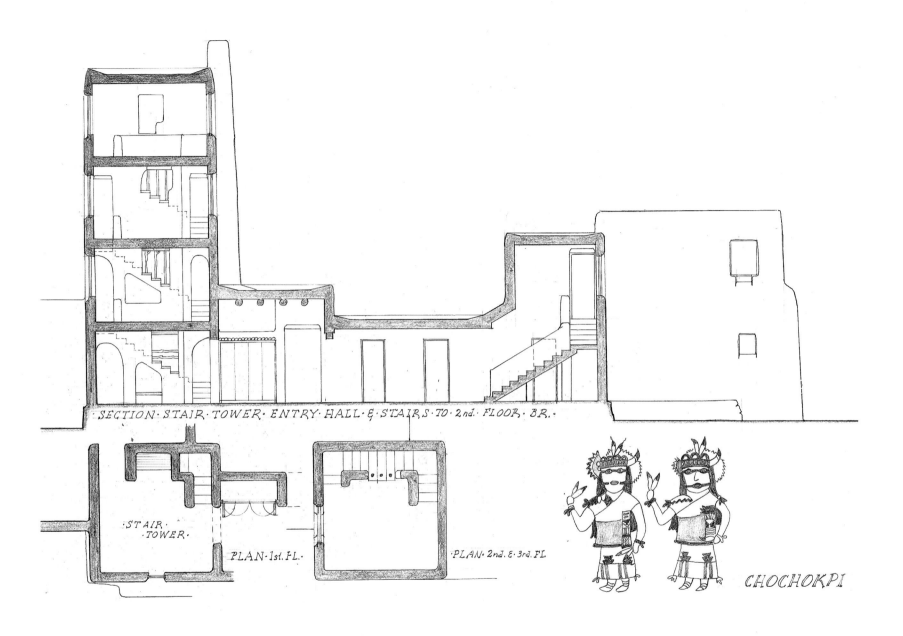

SECTION·STAIR·TOWER·ENTRY·HALL·&·STAIRS·TO·2nd·FLOOR·BR·

·STAIR· TOWER·

PLAN·1st·FL·

·PLAN· 2nd·&·3rd·FL

CHOCHOKPI

PLATE 43. *Throne for the Clouds*

Lumpkins placed the *Throne for the Clouds*—a sitting room—on the top floor of the three-story square tower. This feature dominates the design and is easily accessible from the entranceway to the residence. While there is a living room, the tower itself must function as a special place for guests. The sculptural use of adobe in this design accentuates the hand-built look of the residence.

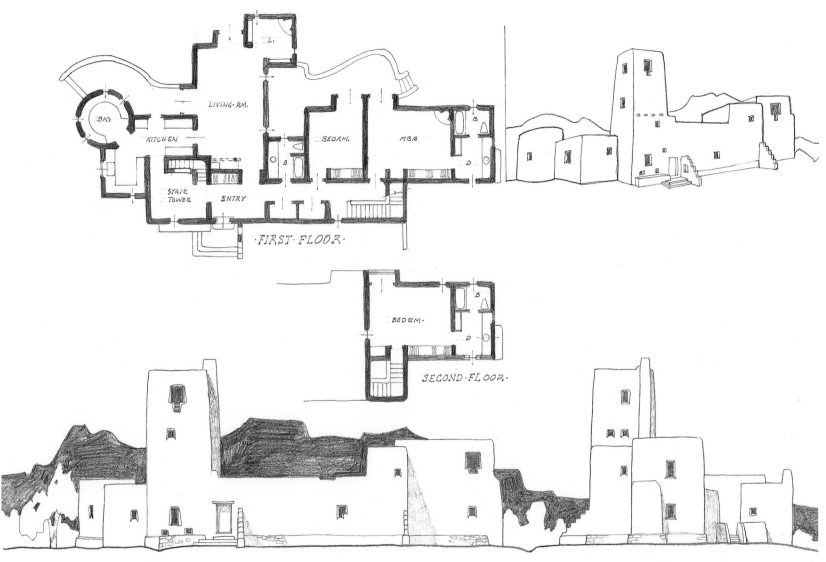

·FIRST·FLOOR·

BK's

LIVING·RM.

KITCHEN

BEDRM.

MBR

B

B

D

STAIR TOWER

ENTRY

A

·SECOND·FLOOR·

BEDRM·

B

D

·FRONT·

·CHOCHOKPI· (THRONE FOR THE CLOUDS)

·PLATE·43·

PLATE 43

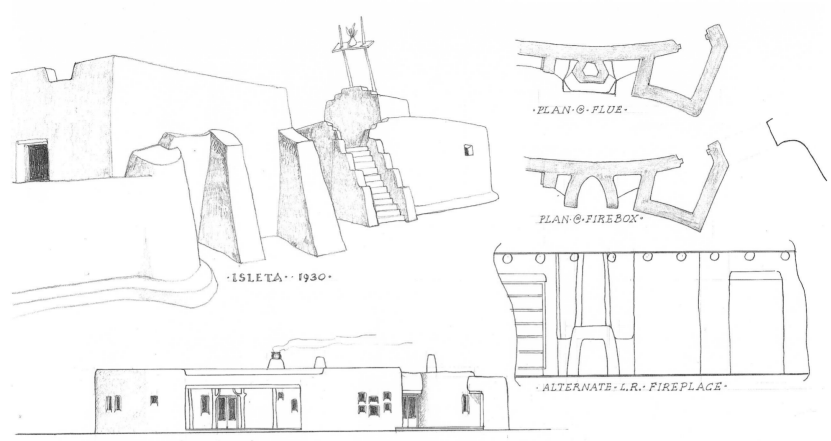

·PLAN·@·FLUE·

·PLAN·@·FIREBOX·

·ISLETA· 1930·

·ALTERNATE·L.R.·FIREPLACE·

·REAR·ELEVATION·

PLATE 44. *Summer Moon*

Summer Moon presents a tightly organized, asymmetrically designed project that emphatically rejects right angles and straight walls. Perhaps the most interesting aspect of the design is the sweeping portal that curves around the rear of the building. The tightness of the design precludes the use of flagstone interior patios to separate areas of the building or to negate the use of walls to separate the interior from the exterior. The sculptural use of adobe adapts the aesthetics of early Pueblo floor plans to modern residential design.

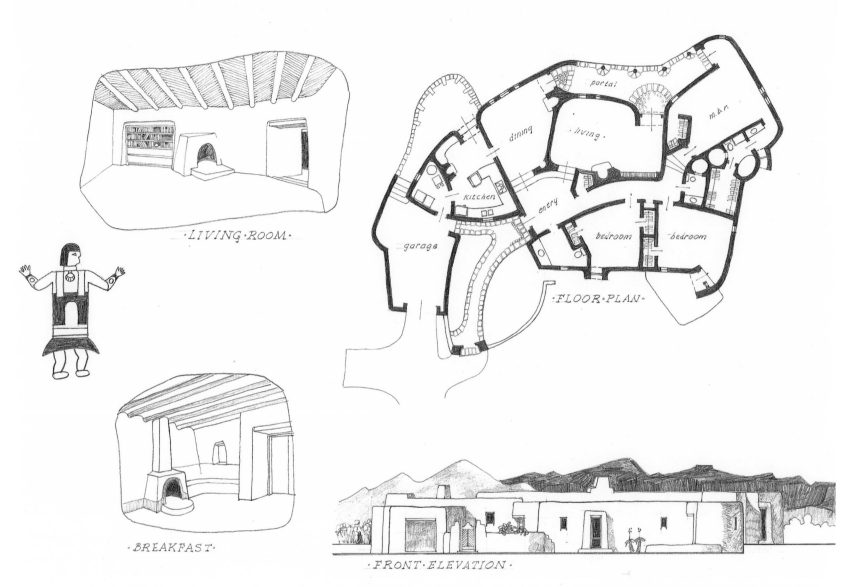

·LIVING·ROOM·

·BREAKFAST·

portal

dining

living

m.b.r.

kitchen

entry

garage

bedroom

bedroom

·FLOOR·PLAN·

·FRONT·ELEVATION·

TALA'MÚ́YAW·
SUMMER·MOON·····PLATE·44

PLATE 44

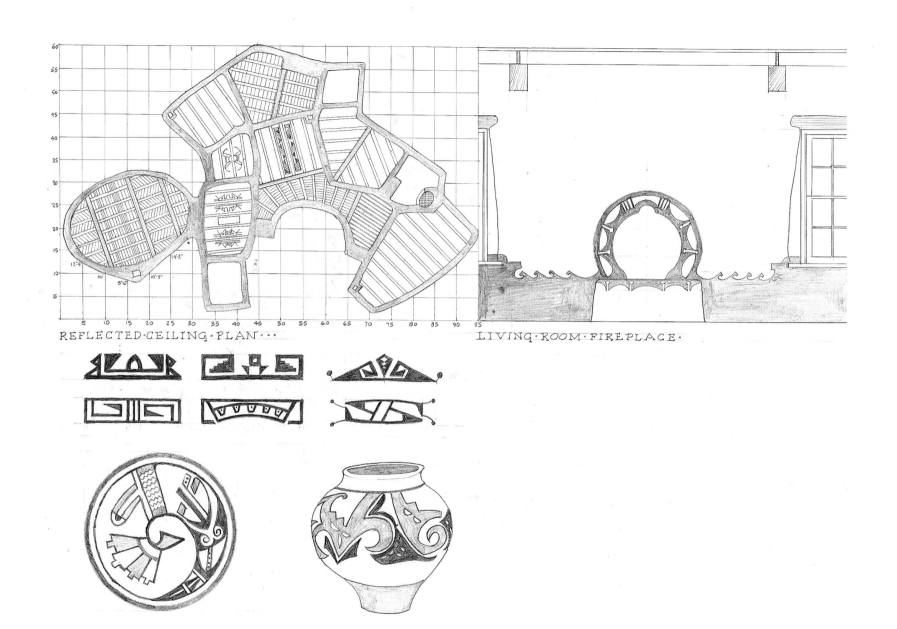

REFLECTED·CEILING·PLAN···

LIVING·ROOM·FIREPLACE·

PLATE 45. *Stars That Cling Together*

Here is another dense, asymmetrical design that basically is circular in form without right angles and straight walls. This project is less compact than Lumpkins's design *Summer Moon* (plate 44) and includes walled patios with flagstones. The patterns of vigas and latillas in the roof structure, shown in the second sheet, define the complexity of this design.

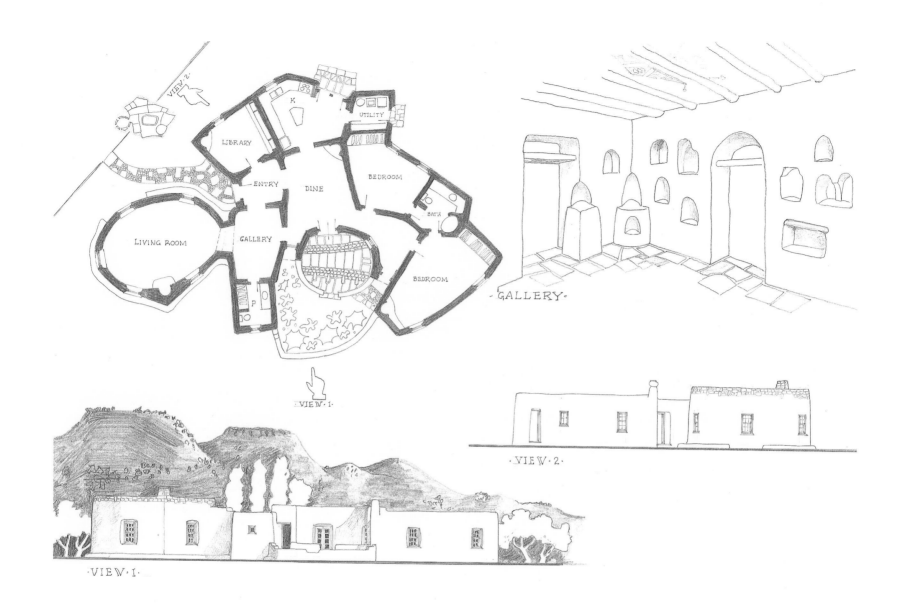

VIEW 2

K

LIBRARY

UTILITY

ENTRY

DINE

BEDROOM

BATH

LIVING ROOM

GALLERY

BEDROOM

P

VIEW 1

GALLERY

VIEW 2

VIEW 1

·CHÖÖCHÖKAM··· STARS·THAT·CLING·TOGETHER
·THE·PLEIADES· PLATE·45

PLATE 45

·PLAN·

·PLAN·AT·FIREBOX·

PLAN·AT·FLUE

PLATE 46. *Fireplaces and Doors*

Lumpkins elaborates on ideas for fireplaces and door details in these two drawings. The fireplaces play a dominant role in the construction of Lumpkins's concept of the living room. Similarly, the graphic placement of panels within the doors serve as another repeated visual device that unifies both interior and exterior spaces. These designs should be considered elaborations for this conceptual series of residences.

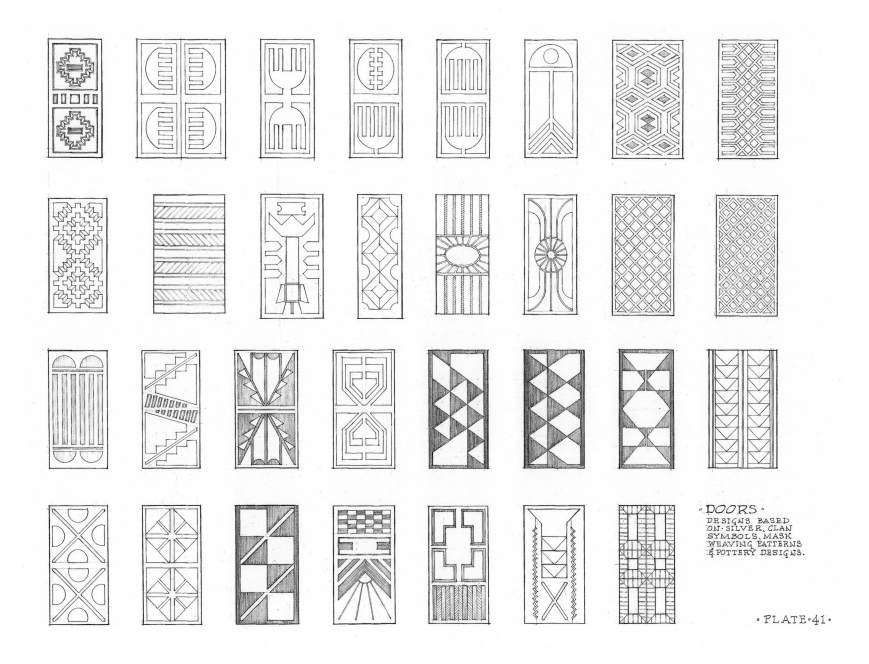

·DOORS·
DESIGNS BASED
ON·SILVER, CLAN
SYMBOLS, MASK
WEAVING PATTERNS
& POTTERY DESIGNS.

·PLATE·41·

PLATE 46

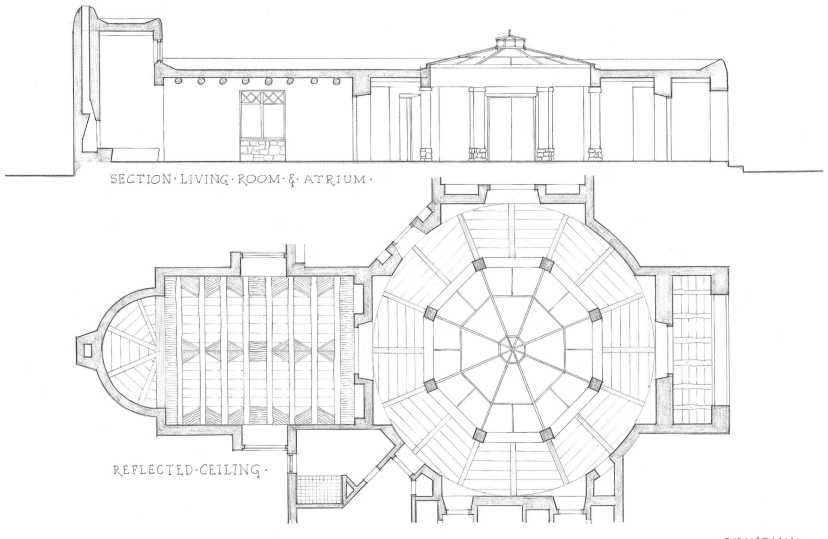

SECTION·LIVING·ROOM·&·ATRIUM·

REFLECTED·CEILING·

CHU'PAWA

PLATE 47. *Corn House*

Lumpkins returns to a formal, one-story residence in *Corn House*. Here he structures the entranceway–atrium–living room series of rooms as the central axis of the design with two wings branching off at right angles. Residents enter the wing of privates spaces from one side of the atrium, while the dining room, library, and kitchen constitute the second wing. The central octagonal atrium features clerestory windows that bring light into this principal space. The adobe exterior is well modeled to soften the geometry of the residence against the landscape.

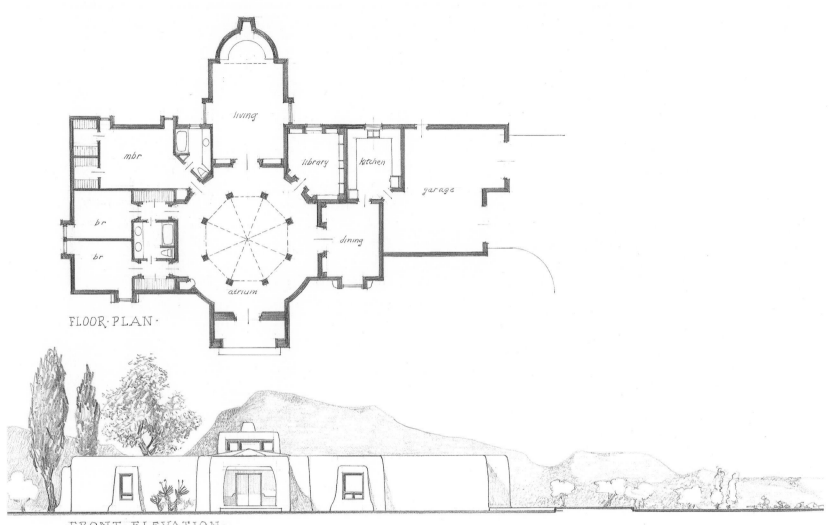

·FLOOR·PLAN·

living

mbr

library   kitchen

garage

br

atrium

dining

br

·FRONT·ELEVATION·

CHU'PAWA··CORN·HOUSE
PLATE·47

PLATE 47

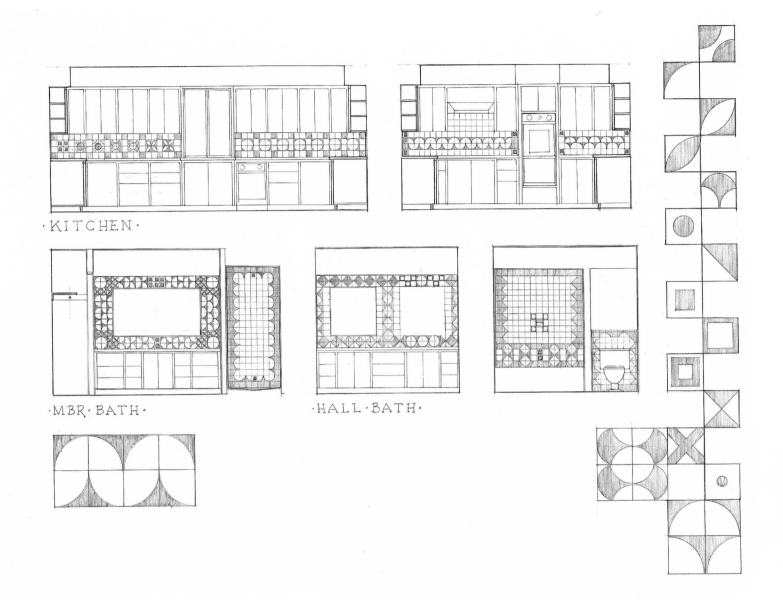

·KITCHEN·

·MBR·BATH·

·HALL·BATH·

PLATE 48. *Kiva Society*

In *Kiva Society*, the final design in this series, Lumpkins reworks his design *Corn House* (plate 47) by substituting a circular atrium. A hallway behind partitions the atrium and connects the private wing of bedrooms with the more public living room and dining room. Internally this formal design seems closely related to Lumpkins's Spanish-Pueblo projects.

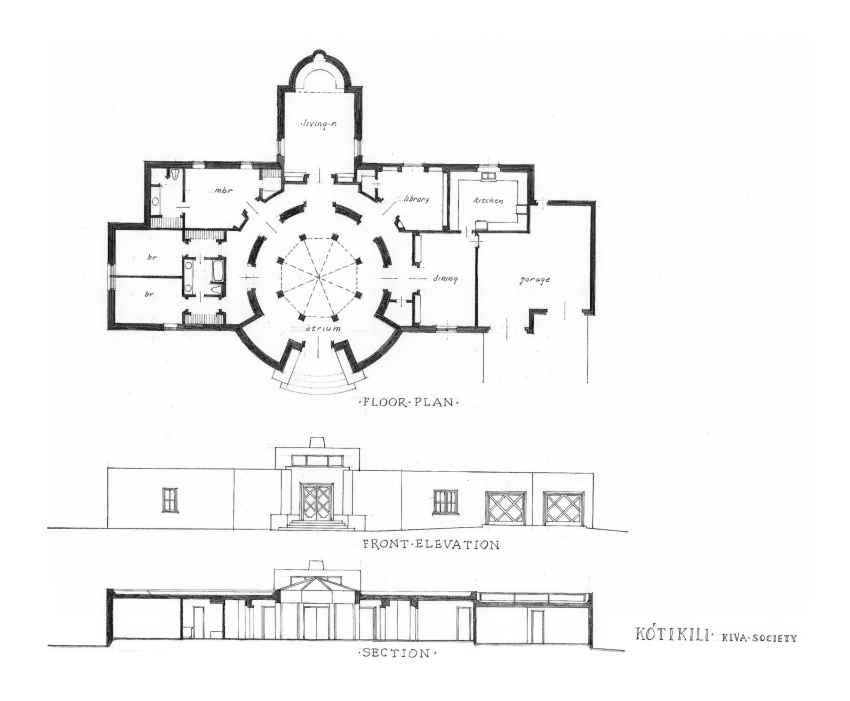

·FLOOR·PLAN·

living·r.

mbr

library

kitchen

br

dining

garage

br

atrium

FRONT·ELEVATION

·SECTION·

KÓTIKILI· KIVA·SOCIETY

PLATE 48

· NOTES ·

INTRODUCTION

1. Gustav Stickley. "The Craftsman Idea," in *Craftsman Homes: Architecture and Furnishings of the American Arts and Crafts Movement* (New York City: Craftsman Publishing Company, 1909; reprint edition, New York: Dover Publications, 1979), 196.

2. Ibid., 201.

3. For a detailed history of revival architecture in New Mexico, see Christopher Wilson's chapter "Romantic Regional Architecture, 1905–1930" in *The Myth of Santa Fe: Creating a Modern Regional Tradition* (Albuquerque: University of New Mexico Press, 1997), 110–145.

4. For plans of Lumpkins's Spanish-Pueblo Designs, see his 1946 *Modern Spanish-Pueblo Homes* (Santa Fe: Western Plan Service, 1946) and his 1961 *La Casa Adobe* (Santa Fe: Ancient City Press, 1961). The designs from *Modern Spanish-Pueblo Homes* do not include enclosed courtyards, while the later plans published in *La Casa Adobe* do.

5. MaLin Wilson includes a biographical interview and a chronology of Lumpkins work as a painter in her catalogue *William Lumpkins: Works on Paper 1930–1986* (Albuquerque: Jonson Gallery, 1987).

6. For a readable travelogue and history that carefully discusses some of the Pueblo ruins of the region, see Sherry Robinson's *El Malpais, Mt. Taylor, and the Zuni Mountains: A Hiking Guide and History* (Albuquerque: University of New Mexico Press, 1994).

7. For information on the archaeology and cultural geography of the El Morro Valley, see Keith W. Kintigh, "Settlement, Subsistence and Society in Late Zuni Prehistory," in *Anthropological Papers of the University of Arizona No. 44* (Tucson: University of Arizona Press, 1985). Details and a site maps of the Kluckhohn Ruin (pp. 40–42) and the Pettit Site (pp. 28–29) are also included.

8. Lumpkins numbered his plates one to forty-eight, each with two sheets. The first sheet in each set often includes a drawing of the source material, while the second sheet emphasizes details and cross-sections. However, plate 33(B), 46(A) and 46(B) are either missing or were never drawn. Similarly, Lumpkins drew two plates numbered 41. The second plate 41, comprised of a single sheet detailing door designs and a sheet of fireplace details, is here numbered plate 46. The titles for these projects come from the Hopi dictionary included in Frank Waters's *Book of the Hopi* (New York: Viking Press, 1963). For simplicity, this study will rely on the English translations. Lumpkins met Waters early in the 1930s and maintained a long friendship with him.

9. In his introduction to Lumpkins's *Casa del Sol: Your Guide to Passive Solar House Design* (Santa Fe: Santa Fe Publishing Company, 1981), 11, Benjamin T. ("Buck"), Rogers notes, "I have long regarded Bill as the Dean of practicing Santa Fe adobe architects."

10. Sarah Nestor discusses vocational and educational training programs in northern New Mexico in *The Native Market of the Spanish New Mexican Craftsman: Santa*

Fe 1933–1940 (Santa Fe: The Colonial New Mexico Historical Foundation, 1978) 12-18. Lumpkins produced "bluebooks" for his students—mimeographed plans of northern New Mexico furniture and woodworking projects. William Wroth reprinted Lumpkins's drawings from the Peñasco area in *Furniture from the Hispanic Southwest* (Santa Fe: Ancient City Press, 1984).

11. Lumpkins published two designs in *Modern Spanish-Pueblo Homes* that he enlarged from his original solar adobe. Lumpkins structured both of these residences—plate 47-12 (pp. 30–31) and plate 47-31 (pp. 68–69) around large, south-facing living rooms featuring solar-gain glass windows shielded under an overhang. These small homes of 853 and 984 square feet represent the modest scale of the time.

12. Lumpkins, *La Casa Adobe*, n.p.

13. Lumpkins trained during the 1930s when renderings constituted an important part of an architect's work. Consequently, he responded positively to reproductions of drawings found in the publications by the Mindeleffs. Lumpkins further simplified these tonal illustrations into contour drawings with heavy shadows.

14. Gustav Stickley. "The Craftsman Idea," in *Craftsman Homes: Architecture and Furnishings of the American Arts and Crafts Movement*, 196.

PLATES

15. Lumpkins bases the multiple levels of *Bear Clan* on John K. Hillers's photograph *Masonry Terraces of Oraibi*, published as plate XXXIX from Victor Mindeleff's "A Study of Pueblo Architecture in Tusayan and Cibola," after 86.

16. H. Hobart Nichols's drawing *Outside Steps at Pescado*, reproduced as plate XCIX from Ibid, after 202, provided the inspiration for Lumpkins's project *On the Slope*.

17. Lumpkins bases *Clan House of Aholi* on a small room block that can be seen in the background of Hillers's photograph *Shumopavi*, reproduced as plate XXXV from Ibid., after 80.

18. Lumpkins bases *Eagle Land* on Hillers's photograph of rooftops at Zuni Pueblo, which Mindeleff published as the halftone engraving *Masonry Chimneys of Zuñi*, plate CI from Ibid., after 206. Hillers's photograph shows the relationship between first-story rooftops and additional stories in the Cibola region.

19. H. Hobart Nichols's drawing *A Covered Passageway in Mashongnavi*, published as plate CIV from Ibid., after 212, provides source material for Lumpkin's drawing *Mishongovi*. The one-point perspective of the Nichols's illustration underscores the photographic source of this pen-and-ink rendering.

20. The source for the fireplace in *Antelope House* is *A Terrace Cooking-pit and Chimney of Walpi*, published as figure 72 from Ibid., 177.

21. *Ground Plan of a Ruin on the Bottom Land in Canyon del Muerto*, figure 2 in Cosmos Mindeleff's "The Cliff Ruins of Canyon de Chelly, Arizona," 96, provides source material for Lumpkins's design *Planting Moon*.

22. Lumpkins developed this see-through concept in *Yellow House* from H. Hobart Nichols's drawing *South Passageway of Walpi*, reproduced as plate XXII in Victor Mindeleff's "A Study of Pueblo Architecture," after 54.

23. In his design *Juniper Leaves* Lumpkins specifically refers to a Zuni fireplace presented as *A Semi-Detached Square Chimney Hood of Zuñi*, figure 65 from Ibid., 172.

24. The inspiration of Lumpkins's project *Sagebrush* is Hillers's classic view of multistory Pueblo architecture that mimics the natural geology of the surrounding landscape. Mindeleff published this image as plate XXI from Ibid., after 52.

25. The Pueblo icons that Lumpkins utilizes in his "T"-shaped doorways are found in figures 84 and 85 from Ibid., 191 and 192 respectively, along with a corner fireplace from figure 67, 174, in the same publication as the icons in his project *Twilight*.

26. The door motifs in Lumpkins's project *Evergreen Village* rely on *A symmetrically notched Doorway in Mashongnavi*, published as figure 83 from Ibid., 190, as an exterior motifs defining the fenestration of the facades.

27. Lumpkins bases his project *Scattered Rocks* on the prehistoric layout found in *Ground Plan of a Small Ruin, No. 44*, published as figure 36 in Cosmos Mindeleff's "The Cliff Ruins of Canyon de Chelly, Arizona," 137.

28. The *Ground Plan of the Upper Part of Casa Blanca Ruin*, published as figure 15 in Ibid., 106, serves as the basis of Lumpkins's project *Water Grass Place*.

29. Lumpkins's project *Circle* presents a symmetrical interpretation of *Ground Plan of a Small Ruin in Canyon de Chelly*, published as figure 3 in Ibid., 96.

30. Formally Lumpkins again relies on *Ground Plan of the Upper Part of Casa Blanca Ruin*, published as figure 15 in Ibid., 106, for the internal relationships within his residence *Rock*. This floorpan was also used by Lumpkins in *Water Grass Place*, plate 27.

31. For source material, see *Ground Plan of a Small Village, Ruin No. 16*, published as figure 27 in Ibid., 129.

32. Lumpkins bases his design *House of the Animal Kingdom* from an anonymous wash drawing *Chimney-like Structure in Mummy Cave Ruins*, published as figure 83 in Ibid., 187.

33. *Earth Painted with Green Plants*, along with *Circle* (plate 28), is based on *Ground Plan of a Small Ruin in Canyon de Chelly*, published as figure 3 in Ibid., 96.

Lumpkins, William. *Modern Spanish-Pueblo Homes*. Santa Fe: Western Plan Service, 1946.

Lumpkins, William. *La Casa Adobe*. Santa Fe: Ancient City Press, 1961.

Lumpkins, William. *Casa del Sol: Your Guide to Passive Solar House Design*. Santa Fe: Santa Fe Publishing Company, 1981.

Mindeleff, Cosmos. "The Cliff Ruins of Canyon de Chelly, Arizona." In *Sixteenth Annual Report of the Bureau of Ethnology to the Secretary of the Smithsonian Institution, 1894–95*. Washington, D.C.: Government Printing Office, 1897, 79-198.

Mindeleff, Victor. "A Study of Pueblo Architecture: Tusayan and Cibola." In *Eighth Annual Report of the Bureau of Ethnology to the Secretary of the Smithsonian Institution, 1886–87*. Washington: Government Printing Office, 1891, 13-228 (reprint edition with an introduction by Peter Nabokov, Washington, D.C., and London: Smithsonian Institution Press, 1989).

Nestor, Sarah. *The Native Market of the Spanish New Mexican Craftsmen: Santa Fe, 1933–1940*. Santa Fe: The Colonial New Mexico Historical Foundation, 1978.

Robinson, Sherry. *El Malpais, Mt. Taylor, and the Zuni Mountains: A Hiking Guide and History*. Albuquerque: University of New Mexico Press, 1994.

Stickley, Gustav. *Craftsman Homes: Architecture and Furnishings of the American Arts and Crafts Movement*. New York: Craftsman Publishing Company, 1909 (reprint edition, New York: Dover Publications, Inc., 1979).

Frank Waters. *Book of the Hopi*. New York: Viking Press, 1963.

Wilson, Chris. *The Myth of Santa Fe: Creating a Modern Regional Tradition*. Albuquerque: University of New Mexico Press, 1997.

Wilson, MaLin. *William Lumpkins: Works on Paper, 1930–1986*. Albuquerque: Jonson Gallery, 1987.

Wroth, William. *Furniture from the Hispanic Southwest*. Santa Fe: Ancient City Press, 1984.